OLA AHLVARSSON

Mindchange

This book is dedicated to anyone who struggles with a mean
and critical inner voice, and my daughter
whose inner voice is her best friend.

Originally published by Fri Tanke (2024)

Aniara Press AB 2024
www.aniara.one
info@aniara.one

Typesetting by Per Gustafsson
www.modernstyle.se

ISBN: 9789189954816

Table of contents

The essence of Mindchange thinking

WHAT IF I told you that the key to living your best life lies not in what happens to you, but in how you talk to yourself about what happens? That's not just positive thinking—it's the foundation of Mindchange thinking, a revolutionary approach to creating lasting happiness and success.

This book you're holding is created to help you improve your life by mastering the art of internal dialogue. Whether you're seeking greater happiness, more fulfilling relationships, enhanced success, or deeper harmony, the path begins with understanding one fundamental truth: how you speak to yourself determines your experience of life.

My journey with Mindchange thinking has led me to both material success and an exciting career, multiple World Championship medals in martial arts, and rewarding relationships with friends and family. More importantly, it has given me something priceless—a beautiful and profound relationship with myself.

The power of Mindchange thinking rests on recent scientific discoveries about the brain's plasticity—its ability to form new pathways and evolve throughout life based on how we use it. Think of your brain as a muscle that grows stronger in the areas you train. This means anyone can enhance their thinking patterns and increase their happiness, regardless of their starting point.

Here's the key insight: everything in our lives—memories, traumas, dramatic events, dreams, and hopes—are (re) created as we interpret them in the present moment, based on how we talk to ourselves about them. This realization is transformative.

It means it's never too late to have a good childhood, never too late to overcome jealousy, never too late to stop being angry in traffic or afraid of snakes.

But this also means you're fully responsible for your own interpretation of the world and for making yourself happy. If this sounds overwhelming or simplistic, know that it's neither. It's simple, but not easy. Like any form of training, you need to do the actual work to get better results. It requires conscious thinking and becoming a master of your emotions rather than their slave.

Living in a world where chance and other people determine your happiness is far more frightening than one where you hold the controls and your happiness is in your hands. To be clear, your past experiences are crucial in explaining why you feel and think the way you do today. Just as your history with exercise and nutrition influences your starting point when you first step into a gym. My point is that anyone can improve their thinking—and therefore their happiness level—regardless of their starting point.

Think about four people walking into a gym for the first time. One is in her forties, somewhat overweight but with a history of athletics; the second is a 75-year-old recovering from a stroke; the third is an 18-year-old karate champion looking to build muscle; and the fourth is you. Each person starts from a different place, but here's what's certain: if they all work out consistently for a year, everyone will be stronger than before. After four years, they'll likely have transformed their physiques entirely.

The same principle applies to Mindchange thinking. Everyone can evolve toward their respective goals, one thought at a time. Just like in the gym, it's about getting into a process of actual practice. The insight itself is just the beginning—like knowing how to do a bench press doesn't automatically build muscle.

The Mindchange model teaches that anyone who wants to

live a harmonious, happy, and successful life can do so by taking ownership of their inner narrative. This frees up enormous mental energy that would otherwise be spent on fear, anger, worry, doubt, self-contempt, or unproductive insecurities. Think of our overweight gym-goer—they know exactly what they need to do for that beach body, but there's work ahead. Not just at the gym, but in their food choices, in choosing to cycle to work with a smile, in passing the candy aisle without impulse buying. Together, these changes in behavior, choices, thoughts, and feelings drive a complete transformation in their relationship with health.

The key difference? While most people know at least the basics of getting fit through exercise, most don't know how to think better or develop their inner voice into a loving, supportive companion. That's where Mindchange thinking comes in.

The Mindchange model and how to interpret the world

THIS CHAPTER WILL give you a comprehensive understanding of the Mindchange Model and the theory behind it. You'll follow my journey and discover how this model has helped me build a beautiful relationship with myself and my own thoughts.

Mindchange is a series of insights that together create a powerful model for transforming how you think. While the impact varies for different readers, this isn't meant to be a treatment method for mental illness or purely theoretical framework. Instead, it draws from cutting-edge scientific research, philosophical wisdom, and concrete understanding of how our brains work. I've refined these insights over many years, working with inspiring thinkers and practitioners from diverse fields.

For me, Mindchange thinking has led to success in terms of material achievements and an exciting career, several World Championship medals in sports, and rewarding relationships with friends and family. More importantly, it has given me something priceless—a beautiful and profound relationship with myself. These are goals most people strive for (and many suffer without). My only mission in sharing these results is to empower others to choose what they need and want—to help more people feel happy and content with their lives and the world around them. Every word is written to share, teach and inspire, not to impress or force anything on anyone.

How we talk to ourselves and interpret the world determines how we think and feel

The fundamental insight underlying the model is simple yet profound: how we speak to ourselves and interpret the world determines how we think and feel.

The model builds on the fact that our brains are plastic—they can be trained and changed (we'll explore brain plasticity in detail, including the revolutionary discovery that our brains develop new pathways throughout life based on stimulation). Your brain is like any muscle that you can develop and expand, becoming more powerful in the areas you train. This is one of the foundational conditions that makes Mindchange thinking work, and we'll return to this theme throughout the book. Contrary to previous beliefs, our brains can not only develop skills but continuously expand their capacity throughout life. This is incredible news because it means everyone can train their thinking and increase their happiness regardless of their starting point—and that includes you.

Everything in our lives takes place in the here and now as electrical impulses travel between our brain cells. This means that all memories, traumas, dramatic events, dreams, and hopes happen as we interpret them from now onwards, based on how we talk to ourselves about them. This insight is transformative. It means it's never too late to have a good childhood, never too late to stop being jealous, never too late to overcome anger in traffic or fear of snakes. But it also means you're fully responsible for your own interpretation of the world and making yourself happy.

If this sounds overly simplistic or scary, know that it's neither.

It's simple, but not easy. Like any form of training, you need to do the actual work to get better results. This requires conscious thinking and becoming a master of your emotions rather than their slave. Think of it as becoming the CEO of a powerful team of emotions working together. Living in a world where chance and other people determine your happiness is far more frightening than one where you hold the controls and your happiness is in your hands.

Positive and negative catalysts

However, just like with physical fitness, mental fitness and conscious thinking can be helped or hindered by factors around you. I call these factors catalysts because they drive thoughts and feelings in either a positive direction (positive catalysts) or negative direction (negative catalysts). Positive catalysts that make it easier to think and act positively include obvious examples like health, friendship, love, family, purpose, and other elements that naturally support positive thinking. Imagine it's the first day of your summer vacation and you're heading to meet someone who's captured your heart—it's easier to notice flowers and butterflies, think happy thoughts, and love life.

But there are also negative catalysts that can pull you into loops of frustration, doom, and gloom. To identify negative catalysts, you can often look at a positive catalyst and flip it around. If being healthy and sleeping well makes positive thinking easier, then sleep deprivation and an unhealthy lifestyle likely act as negative catalysts. If having meaningful purpose brings joy, then lacking purpose can trigger sadness and meaninglessness. If love is a positive catalyst, then lack of love can certainly be a negative catalyst leading to loneliness and sadness.

Your world view and other chosen truths

It's also crucial to understand the chosen truths that guide your meaning-making and worldview, which is why we'll explore spirituality, philosophy, and other chosen truths (I use the word "chosen" because, as you'll see, they're a choice, not a given fact). These chosen truths, combined with your positive and negative catalysts, create the story you tell yourself—and this story is crucial in determining your levels of happiness and fulfillment. Think of it as your default setting, similar to how a phone or computer comes with factory settings before you personalize it with your own configurations and programs. Similarly, Mindchange thinking can transform your world of thought and feeling, regardless of your default setting.

What about your previous experiences?

As mentioned earlier, we're greatly influenced by past experiences and how life has treated us in terms of how easy or difficult it is to embrace disciplined thinking and become masters of our emotions. What I find empowering is that no matter where you come from, it's not about going backwards but rather about creating the story that will make you happy in the future. (And again, I'm not discussing extreme experiences or mental illness, although Mindchange thinking can help there too, as my paralyzed father proved every day.)

A model is a model is a model

Each model is a simplification of complex reality, just like a map between Los Angeles and New York simplifies the actual road, landscape, flora, fauna, people, traffic, buildings, and everything else along the way. Just as the map doesn't claim to be the real 1:1 experience, the Mindchange model doesn't claim to handle all situations, work identically for everyone, or manage the vast complexity of human thinking. However, like a good map, the model's quality should be judged by how well it helps you reach your destination.

I've been fascinated by philosophy since falling in love with the subject in college. I've spent my life as an amateur explorer of thought systems, constantly seeking to understand how we humans work. One American philosopher who's inspired me is John Dewey and his school of pragmatism. For Dewey, philosophy and ideas have no value in themselves. Their value comes from helping people and societies make better decisions and evolve through new ways of thinking and making meaning. A model, theory, or hypothesis gains its value when it's experienced and makes things better. If such a model is found, education becomes crucial to spread the new, better system of thinking. I deeply appreciate Dewey's approach, believing that what our time needs most is better systems of thought for both individuals and societies.

Society and our lack of a common narrative

The absence of religion in many secular societies creates a void as priests no longer serve as counselors and a divine being no longer watches over increasingly lonely souls facing certain death without purpose. On the other end of the spectrum, practitioners of traditional religions watch the role of God shrinking as weather apps replace prayers for good weather, and it becomes impossible to shield children from the internet's temptations as our exponentially evolving world collides faster and more definitively with old dogmas and orthodox belief systems.

Meanwhile, family structure and parenting are shifting from the old proverb "it takes a village to raise a child" to just trying to "make the life puzzle work," leaving many children struggling in unhealthy family dynamics where "family" no longer provides the sanctuary of continuity it once did.

The multicultural, subcultural, international, and changing aspects of modern society make it impossible to sit back and let culture guide you through life's decisions, unlike tribal or ancient societies where culture provided context and belonging while severely limiting available choices. This increasingly complex reality, with fewer philosophical, religious, cultural, and familial structures to support our personal development, creates a void leading to unhappiness and frustration on a global scale. Depression rates are climbing, psychotropic drug use is at historic highs, and polarization becomes the norm as masses search for meaning by following clickbait and populist extremists.

Against this backdrop, we clearly need a new narrative that can help individuals, businesses, and societies become better at creating happiness. But as Dewey would argue, the models that thinkers and philosophers create must be tested in the real world—and only when they work should they be scaled up.

Is this just another self-help book where you learn to talk to yourself?

There's a whole field of books promising to accelerate well-being and personal development through quick fixes. But life isn't a quick fix. Life is literally what you have to live with for the rest of your life. This book's purpose isn't to fix your life, but to help you transform your approach to living by becoming more aware of how you react and relate to the world around you. The ambition is to offer a thinking system I've found valuable, bringing together common traits I've identified in science, personal experience, and as shared characteristics of harmonious, happy people.

The self-help field is saturated with pseudo-scientific grand promises and oversimplifications. It's a term that, I would argue, diminishes a school of thought that has the bold ambition of helping you realize how to embrace disciplined thinking and understand much more about the art and science of thinking well and living a good life. Labeling the Bible or Aristotle's works as self-help just because they both address life's biggest questions would only place them on the wrong shelf in the bookstore rather than positioning them as valuable companions through life. Without any other comparison to these masterpieces, I hope the same will apply to this book and related content.

Mindchange is for everyone

As you become more familiar with the model, you'll realize it can accommodate almost any belief system, chosen truth, and way of life without judging or forcing change. It's neutral to good and bad in the sense that successful Mindchanging leads the practitioner to live a better life both in the short and long term. For some, this may mean leaving their Christian faith behind and becoming a devout atheist. For someone else, it may be finding Allah or Jesus and true meaning and joy in this life (and beyond?). The thought process is in this sense agnostic to the underlying belief system and therefore useful to everyone regardless of worldview.

In simple terms, the model means the following:

"How you talk to yourself, how you interpret the world around you and within you, and what your (chosen) truths are, will dictate how happy and fulfilled your life is."

It also says that you can make the process of talking better to yourself easier or harder depending on the positive and negative catalysts in your life. If you're homeless and trying to sleep and it's cold, it's harder to think positively than when your beloved friends throw you a surprise party at your favorite restaurant. But Mindchange thinking is needed more in the former than in the latter example and that is why it is so important to continuously train your thought process. This also means that existing findings in psychology or even astrology (a "science" I have trouble coming to terms with) can be true in the sense that they are powerful catalysts for thought and action and therefore can be perceived as true.

Kind of like someone going to the gym because they want to feel fit and by doing so actually feeling fit and good looking afterwards. According to the Mindchange Theory, they could have gone straight to thinking they are fit through disciplined thought and skipped the gym. This phenomenon can be seen in

TV shows like The Biggest Loser where it's clear that you don't have to be fit to feel fit, just more fit than you were before. When you understand that you create the thoughts yourself, you realize that being "fit" or "good-looking" are not objective statements, but rather mental constructs.

Your journey ahead starts here. This book consists of several parts that will guide you through understanding and implementing Mindchange thinking in your own life. We'll explore everything from the basic theory to practical applications, from understanding your default settings to creating new, more empowering mental patterns. Let's begin.

Your journey ahead

This book consists of several parts, where in the first part I invite you to understand the Mindchange Theory and how the brain works in broad terms. The second part is dedicated to understanding the default setting we all have and the positive and negative catalysts that consciously or unconsciously influence our ability to think better. Then we make the insights practical by seeing how they relate to some of the issues that usually top everyone's list, such as love, success, family but also how to deal with emotions like fear, anger, lack of meaning and many other recurring themes that cause many to suffer. This is followed by chapters based on practical applications of the Mindchange model where I share spells that have worked magic in my life and that I hope will be useful to many readers and listeners. To delve deeper into each topic, I've created videos linked to the chapters that can be viewed by scanning the QR code or visiting mindchanged.com.

What if this is true?

> "I believe that this unhappiness is largely due to wrong perceptions of the world, wrong ethics, wrong habits of living, leading to the destruction of the natural desire and appetite for possible things on which all happiness, whether of humans or animals, ultimately depends."
>
> - The Conquest of Happiness, Bertrand Russell

We spend half of our waking hours talking to ourselves. If you think about it, you know this to be true, yet there are few guidelines or teachers to show us how to do this well, or how to avoid truly destructive inner communication. We are leaving tradition, religion and duty behind and entering a world where everyone needs to learn to think and where there are few genuine gurus, but hordes of charlatans who prey on believers and deceive those who are lost and willing to pay to find something to believe in within our complicated world.

By now you probably know that the main message of this book is: How you feel depends on how you talk to yourself. What if this is true? What if it really is up to you to make yourself feel successful, beautiful, excited and confident? Wouldn't that be amazing? Can you imagine all the worries and frustrations that you would have avoided throughout your life? The unnecessary heartache and disappointments. The sour taste of failure or defeat turned into... well, whatever you want.

Why is this important?

The world around us is changing faster than ever, and the choices facing most people today are more complex than in societies of the past. Previously, class, culture and religion determined to a greater extent what to think and how to act. Additionally, everyday life left little time for existential concerns beyond just trying to stay alive and look after family In many ways life was much harder to live in the past. It is therefore strange and worrying that our improved living conditions, with better healthcare systems, social welfare systems, education, freedom and greater respect for the individual have led to... more depression.

Quality of life is lost for people who feel unhappy, lack meaning or, worse, fall into clinical depression. Mental health problems lead to a spiral of worsening thoughts and poor decisions that deepen depression or health problems.

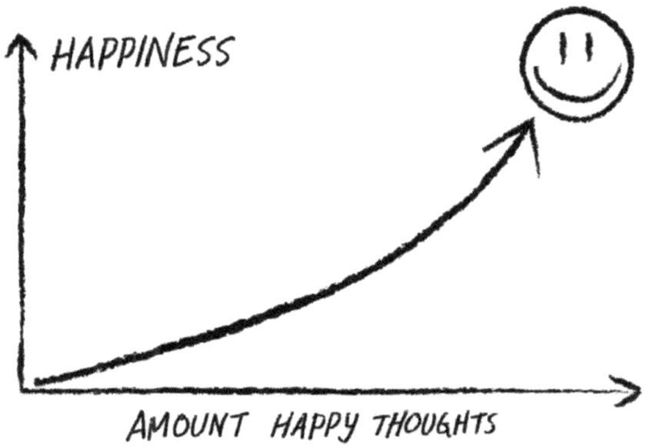

Why should you be happy?

According to Professor Micael Dahlen and his wonderful A Little Book on Happiness, happier people are healthier, live longer, make other people happier, are more successful and, curiously, receive shorter prison sentences in court. In short, happy people live better lives.

This is also true for organizations where fearless, happy and satisfied employees do a much better job, make better use of the skills and creativity of the whole team and create greater job satisfaction than in a workplace where employees are unhappy.

Summary

- How you feel depends on how you talk to yourself.
- You can train how to talk to yourself better because the brain is plastic (and works much like a muscle and nothing happens if you don't train).
- The world is becoming increasingly complex and we are less supported in how to deal with this complexity, which leads to anxiety and unhappiness. Mindset thinking can help you relate to the world in a way that makes you happy because it is how you interpret the world that determines how you feel.
- Everyone can be happier and more harmonious through Mindchange thinking.

A metaphor to take away from Chapter 1:

The brain loves stories and storytelling as we will see in the next chapters. Therefore, when applicable, I will end with a fairy tale that can help you remember the message of the chapter.

Imagine that you dream that you are in a beautiful garden and there you meet a fairy who says: "Welcome here, I've been waiting for you. This is the garden of your happiness, isn't it beautiful?" You look out over the garden and see flowers, young trees gently reaching for the sky, but also weeds growing unhindered, sucking nutrients from the soil and the other plants. When you look closely at the flowers, you see that they represent the joys of your life. You rejoice in the apple tree that represents the love of your children, a flower your favourite hobby, a beautiful rose the tranquillity of your summer place. You are filled with joy and gratitude when you see the beauty of the garden. But you also realise that the weeds represent negative things in your life. The wild thistles symbolise your job that you hate, the dandelions your body that you don't like, and the stinging nettles remind you how lonely you often feel without a companion... all at once, the feelings of happiness disappear and blow away in a whirlwind of anxiety where the inner voice becomes increasingly judgmental and critical. You are pulled out of your negative thoughts by the fairy who hands you a shovel and a jug of water. She smiles and says: "It's easy for anyone to understand how to create a great garden but it requires constant care and nourishment. The first thing to do is to take this shovel and remove all the weeds. Look carefully, some weeds might actually be a flower that you like. Once you've done that, water the flowers and trees. Once you have a garden free of weeds that steal nutrients, and you have spent time and care on all the plants that make you happy, you can plant whatever seeds you like. Don't forget to water them and make sure that no new weeds get a foothold in your garden and your happy garden will become more and more beautiful."

As in the dream, Mindchange thinking starts with your current 'happiness mix' or default setting. The next step is to actually identify what the negative (for example, alcohol abuse or being in a destructive relationship) and positive catalysts (for example, exercise and loving your friends) are. Once you see your 'garden' for what it is, you can analyse and challenge the negative catalysts step by step, weeding out the weeds. The next step is to develop the positive catalysts and 'water' the flowers and trees. This is where the real work of change begins and becomes exciting. Because when you get rid of negative catalysts, you get more energy to create new positive catalysts and can "sow new seeds" that lead to even more happiness and harmony if you continuously keep the weeds in check and don't forget to nourish the garden.

Thoughts to reflect on

Think about what makes you happy and what you enjoy doing and then what makes you sad and what you don't enjoy doing. Can you do more of what you like and less of what you don't like?

What are the negative and positive catalysts in your life, i.e. conditions that make you unhappy or happy on an ongoing basis?

What 'chosen truths' do you have that affect your happiness?

My path to Mindchange

I GREW UP in a loving home with two wonderful parents and an equally wonderful older brother who, like most older brothers, sometimes made life challenging and occasionally practiced management by fear, wielding the power of muscles two years more developed than mine.

Like most children, I was afraid of the dark when I went to bed (but not if my parents were around). I feared the older bullies when I started school and worried whether my big brother and his friends would let me play with them. Later in my youth, I worried about not being popular, thought school was a drag, was devastated when Gunilla in class 6B probably didn't love me back, and agonized over whether my favorite hockey team would win.

During puberty, I desperately wanted to be more mature and manly than I felt or looked in the mirror. I often felt like an impostor, convinced people would like me less if they knew my inner fears and inadequacies. I tried to compensate with fake confidence (I hereby apologize to my friends from that time for being difficult and a pain). I was an average student, managing decent grades only because of my intelligence, memory, and the solid general education I'd received from my parents. In high school, I started drinking, smoking (even trying weed occasionally), and being "bad" became cool. Hating school and established institutions was the norm among my friends in Hallonbergen. I was different from them because I lived in a villa in the upper-middle-class neighborhood of Ursvik in Sundbyberg but went to school in the "Hallonbergen hood" where most kids were less fortunate.

I lived in a culture where you were supposed to be against society and have role models who didn't care about having any ambition, but two things changed my mind and influenced my future more positively than anything else.

In 1977, Gary Gygax, a nerd in Michigan, invented a new board game. He called it Dungeons & Dragons, and it was revolutionary. It was an interactive storytelling experience where you, the player, were the star of a fantasy saga developed collaboratively. Creative interactive stories or 'adventures' were told with a Game Master or Dungeon Master leading the game, along with intricate dice rolls that added unpredictability to every decision. A neighbor boy received a copy of the first version before moving from Michigan to Ursvik, my little unknown hometown.

I'll never forget the absolute feeling of presence as we conquered mystical lands and defeated evil (or good) dragons. Explaining Dungeons & Dragons to someone who's never played is like trying to describe what it's like to be a parent to a ten-year-old. They think they understand, but have no idea how deep the emotions and involvement go. For me, at seven years old, it was an endless canvas for creating worlds, telling stories, leading groups of older children on adventures, learning English (otherwise you couldn't read the books), and developing reading and writing skills. Years later, I realized that role-playing was crucial in making me a storyteller, working with abstract visions, making listeners see and feel what I wanted them to experience, and dealing with both failures and endless imaginary victories.

The second and more important thing that happened was meeting my teacher and second father (my biological father's own words), the Japanese karate master Sensei Iryo Kanenobu, 9th Dan. We met when I was a lost 14-year-old attending Hallonberg School, smoking various substances, skipping class, and living far below my potential. At this age, it's tough for parents to connect because they represent exactly what the teenager rebels against.

I wanted to practice martial arts after watching Bruce Lee films and because I hung out with much older friends. Being a late bloomer, short, and refusing to cut my long blonde hair didn't make things easier. Being mistaken for a girl wasn't the observer's fault, despite my hormonal reactions. I wanted to train martial arts but knew almost nothing about it. I didn't want anyone to know I was training, so practicing in my neighborhood wasn't an option. This would be my secret superpower. The obvious choice would have been the coolest Taekwondo school in town, but instead, I chose to take the bus and train to Sollentuna (my parents also drove and picked me up often). I chose karate, and it turned out to be one of the best decisions of my life. The Taekwondo school became a virtual factory for creating Swedish and international champions, but unfortunately, many youngsters there ended up as professional criminals. The infamous Swedish "Eagle Gang" formed during this time, and all its members were my age and started training at the same Taekwondo club.

When I chose karate, I also chose to become a student of Sensei Iryo. His karate wasn't a sport, and his dojo (training hall) was a haven of kindness, discipline, philosophy, and training in the tradition of shin-gi-tai, Japanese for body, mind, and technique. In his dojo, I began my martial arts career cleaning floors, meditating, performing boring repetitive movements until my body ached and my mind learned patience. Somewhere along the line, I began to focus my energy. Our relationship became very similar to that between the Karate Kid and Mr. Miyagi. My grades rose even faster than my belt colors. I replaced my long hair with a short cut and swapped smoking for interval training, with Sensei cheering me on. Sensei was the first adult male I chose as my role model, allowing him to influence my thoughts and mental development.

In Sensei Iryo's teachings, everyone holds equal value, with kindness and respect at the core of all actions and thoughts. But Sensei is also a demanding teacher who pushes the limits of physical endurance and teaches you to reach potential you never imagined possible. This applies not just to karate but to anything you choose to do passionately. For me as a teenager, this was exactly what I needed, and my wannabe samurai self absorbed the wisdom, techniques, and endorphins that pumped after every practice.

I often wonder what would have happened if I'd gone to the other school instead, training and socializing six days a week with future criminals. Sadly, I think I would have followed their path, which led to many years in prison for several of them. (Most eventually became successful, harmonious adults - a testament to their inner strength.) Many, oddly enough, have also become famous actors and remain my friends.

Sensei and I have maintained and strengthened this relationship throughout my life, with him in my corner when I fought world champions in several martial arts disciplines. He's been a constant presence in my inner dialogue and moral compass. Together we've traveled the world, lived and trained with Shaolin Temple monks, studied with the highest-ranked karate masters in Okinawa, trained in Thai boxing camps, and embarked on countless other adventures in our quest to learn more about martial arts and life. His motto, which we've adopted at the Epicenter innovation house I co-founded, is "I am the only student, everyone else is my teacher." It's a beautiful way to view your fellow humans and a challenge to learn from everyone instead of polarizing or judging. His playful mind combined with commitment to excellence has inspired me for life. I remember countless great moments that proved his unique worldview. Like when I came to train and it was pouring rain, he cheerfully shouted "Look Ola-San, liquid sunshine!" and insisted we train in the park, ending up with something more like mud wrestling than karate. "Our Dojo is everywhere, Ola-San!"

For Sensei, the mind controlled whether the weather was a terrible downpour or liquid sunshine. This simple way of controlling your reality perfectly illustrates this book's message. (As I've said, simple and easy aren't the same thing.) Only our perceptions determine whether we're practicing in a mud pile or in our dojo created by nature. The story becomes even funnier knowing that his daughter's new boyfriend, arriving to meet the parents for dinner, reported seeing two crazy homeless guys fighting in the mud.

Sensei has been present for many of life's most important moments, including presiding over my wedding ceremony and witnessing my 2021 Swedish Championships victory at age 51 against a 24-year-old MMA champion. I write with a heavy heart that Sensei passed away on November 5, 2022, after an unfair battle with pancreatic cancer.

Learning of his pancreatic cancer was one of the hardest blows I've ever received. He had been with me in spirit since my teenage years and throughout adulthood, and I'm not exaggerating when I say he was my main moral compass. I imagine most Christians have a similar relationship with Jesus, who is always with them in spirit. He was also my mentor and source of infinite wisdom. This mentorship developed into a father-son-like love and eternal friendship.

When I realized he was dying, I felt an intense fear of being alone in my head without him (I hope that description resonates with readers). When I expressed this fear, he smiled and said: "Why do you think that? Of course, I will always be there as a sounding board when you need me." I realized with complete clarity that he was right. He would remain with me because I had welcomed my mentor as my eternal companion and observer's perspective guide. He was the inspiration, but I had created the dialogue myself and could continue doing so.

I've created an AI companion to this book whom I call Sensei, who understands Mindchange thinking deeply. He will answer your questions about the book or any thoughts you have as a tribute to the role he played and still plays in my mental dialogue (see www.mindchanged.com).

Sensei wasn't afraid to die. For him, death wasn't the end but the beginning of an exciting new journey. For anyone who has sat beside a dying friend, it's clear that their beliefs and thoughts about what happens next determine their state of mind. Some die screaming while others are excited that the next adventure begins. We'll return to this in detail in the chapter on death.

Martial arts was my gateway to understanding how the brain works and how to control fears and inner dialogue, leading to the transformative insights I hope to share in this book. When training for a full-contact fight, you know you'll get beaten up and risk permanent injury or worse. You also risk hurting another human who, like you, believes the thrill outweighs the risk. Preparing for years for upcoming matches and their risks meant dealing with intense stress - or simply put, fear. (Fear of injury, fear of failing, fear of pain, etc., and being unable to discuss that F-word with the team because we're all tough, fearless fighters.) This forced me to face my fears more than most people.

After years of developing my inner dialogue, I began to

realize many techniques were universal and could combine with discoveries in psychology and other schools of thought to significantly improve quality of life. I felt I had an opportunity, perhaps even a responsibility, to share these findings and help others improve their inner dialogue.

Here's an episode describing the days leading up to and including becoming the 1997 World Kickboxing Champion in Dubrovnik.

Dubrovnik 1997, World Kickboxing Championships, final 69kg

THE SIX GAMES I fought through yesterday make my whole body ache. Every step I take hurts. Really hurts. A crowd of over 5,000 people screaming. I feel sick with nervousness. What the hell am I doing here? Why can't I just sit in a chair at ringside and scream and shout like everyone else?

Yesterday was magical. National team members from all over the world paraded by, proudly waving their country's flag. All proud, all used to be number one. All winners with their sights set on gold. To never give up and to get to the top of their sport.

My first match was against a tough fighter from Belarus. The match was close. He took the lead by giving me a hard kick in the head. I felt like I was losing. Losing in kickboxing is very different from losing in table tennis or most other sports. Each blow feels like the final defeat. I stood up and after a series of punch and kick combinations, the referee raised my hand and I moved on to the next match.

A martial arts tournament is strikingly Darwinian. Not because the strongest wins, which is a common misunderstanding of Darwin's thesis, but because the fighter who can adapt to different opponents and conditions has the best chance of winning. Survival of the fittest. A starting field of national champions is decimated by half after each match. 62 becomes 31, then 16, 8, 4 and finally the two fighters who have made it to the final. During the competition, my mind is working at full speed trying to analyze the other fighters while hoping the best get knocked out by someone else (they never do and you are next to fight them). I then had a clear win against a Slovenian, an Icelander and a Canadian on my way to the semi-finals. So far, my draw had been very fortunate. The starting fields are split into two pools and most of the A nations fought in the second pool while as mentioned above I had Belarus, Iceland, Slovenia and less experienced fighters.

In the semi-final I was up against an Italian who was ranked 4 in the world and who had just won the European Championships. In the other semi-final, Hungary's best kickboxer in all categories, Istvan Toth, faced a hard-hitting mean Russian who had demolished all previous opponents without too much effort and who seemed unstoppable. I knew that if I couldn't grow with the opportunity, the match against the Italian would be a short story. Modern man is rarely exposed to physical danger. Fortunately, we rarely have to fight, run, or survive an antagonist's blows. For those who have never experienced this, it is difficult to understand the mixture of fear, doubt, survival instinct and stress that fighting in the ring brings. Or the adrenaline rush that makes bungee jumping feel like playing bingo, followed by aggression and ambition that harnesses years of training and turns the flight instinct into full battle mode. Some things are not logical. Here I am, of my own free will, standing in front of someone who has devoted his life to kicking and punching and giving him carte blanche to do just that to me. The bell rings for what will be one of the best fights of my life. My opponent rushes out like a bull and tries to end the match quickly. I rely on good footwork and follow up with precision punches and kicks on my increasingly frustrated opponent. We clinch and trade punches. We feint, change tactics and keep a frenzied pace, knowing that whoever goes at full speed will make it to the World Championship final.

The Italian charges forward and I meet him with a jumping spinning back kick that hits him full force. I see him lift off the ground and collapse on the mat hard with both hands clutched to his stomach. I run to the neutral corner and the referee starts counting. The Italian moves his hands to his groin and says it was an illegal kick to the bollocks. Everything is allowed in war and love, but not in kickboxing. Our coaches scream, the audience boos. The referee stops counting and gives the Italian time to recover. I try to send him a contemptuous grin while catching my breath. Both he and I know he would have been KO'd had he not cheated.

The fight continues, the aggression and intensity increases. In the final round, all the pieces fall into place and I float through the motions, much like when Obi-Wan Kenobi in Star Wars tells young Luke to use the force and he finally gets it. A flurry of clean hits and two perfect kicks to the head later and I had won the semi-final and was in the World Championship final. The pain comes a second after the adrenaline has stopped rushing in my veins. A second later, shit I have one more match.

In the second semi-final, the Hungarian Toth loses, and he loses big. The Russian looks too big for our weight class, kicks and punches very hard and has a pace that not only impresses me. It scares me. How the hell am I supposed to keep up with that monster? Besides, he seems to be an arsehole. He has a gimmick of not shaking hands with his opponents before or after the fight and after his semi finals win he shakes a gloved fist at me, points and shouts something in Russian. I try to look cool and unaffected but in my brain a mantra roars on repeat, "what the hell am I doing here". I'm not even particularly interested in sport. My real heroes have never been in the sports arenas. They are the change-makers and entrepreneurs who shape the world around us. "What the hell am I doing here?"

The final is set for the evening of the following day. That means I have to kill over 24 endless hours before getting back in the ring. I only want to eat bananas and some fruit because I'm worried that the local food might make me sick or make my stomach turn. Every inch of my body aches. Even my "weapons", my feet, shins and hands are bruised and swollen. Wherever I go, people pat me on the back and wish me luck, I sign autographs for children and get advice from other fighters. I see in their eyes that no one believes I will have a chance against the Russian. Through the fear and fuelled by their doubts, I begin to feel something else, a budding fire that nourishes a will to fight, to win, to prove them wrong. I find strength in my abilities and in winning the matches that took me to the final.

If I lose tomorrow, I will be number 2. Number 2 is the first loser, as the American saying goes. If I win, my future grandchildren will be able to boast that their grandfather was a world champion. Swedish boxer Ingmar "Ingo" Johansson was world champion and became a hero to the people, would it have been the same if he had been number 2?

I have seen the same fervour in many entrepreneurs. Long after the money or applause was the driving force, they still want to strive for even higher goals. The ancient Greeks believed it was divine fire transmitted by the Titan Prometheus fuelling the ambitions.

The 24 hours before the championship final were some of the worst of my life. I learnt then that there are 60 boring seconds in a minute and 60 of those even more boring minutes in every hour. I woke up at 6am on match day after only a couple of hours of fitful sleep. Every time I moved, I woke up. I often woke up from punching or kicking in my sleep.

At 7am I started a strange walk and walked around, mostly in circles for the next six hours without leaving my hotel room.

Now it's only minutes before the start of the match. TV cameras from international sports channels are all around me as

I fasten my shin guards and bandage my knuckles. A beautiful hostess in a red evening dress holding a sign with my name is supposed to add to the "gala feeling" and the rhythmic applause and stamping of the crowd reaches a crescendo. Suddenly it is as if time stands still. Why the hell am I doing this? I want to walk away or, like Forrest Gump, run away without stopping. Or at least move the fight a few days. My coach looks me deep in the eyes. As if he is saying "if you win this match, you will be proud for the rest of your life". He believes in me.

The moment I enter the ring and see my one head taller opponent staring at me with adrenaline filled eyes, his black mouth guard and a yellow and blue-black eye, I enter "the zone". All doubts are gone and so are the pain and thoughts. In its place takes a cold confidence, years of training and a firm conviction that it is my hand that will be raised by the judge.

The match starts evenly. We exchange punches and kicks and feel each other out. I feel like I'm winning the first round but get a hard right to the face in the second and go down. The referee starts counting. I remember thinking, "stay down, then it's over and silver in the World Championships isn't bad", then I regain my determination and I stand up and am more focused on winning than before. The dance continues. Raw strength versus technical finesse. He hits harder, I am more creative and technical.

When the match is finally over, we both raise our hands to the sky to declare who is the winner. My coach runs into the ring with the rest of the Swedish team and lifts me up. I hear the crowd shouting my name from a distance. The head referee clears the ring of everyone except me and the Russian. He grabs our wrists. Judge one, Russian victory. Judge two, Swedish victory. Judge three, Swedish victory. Judge four, Russian victory. My brain is spinning even faster than my beating heart. The last and final judge scores the fight and the new world kickboxing champion,

Dubrovnik 1997, World Kickboxing Championships, final 69kg

Olaaaa Ahlvarsoooon, Sweden.

That moment ended the first part of my martial arts career and the moment my hand was raised I said, this is it. No more fights (I was wrong). The day after our venture, Boxman received 17 million in funding from top investors and a new chapter began in my life. A chapter that would take me around the world as an entrepreneur, starting more than 20 companies over the next decades. But first, let's go back to where it all began. My parents.

My Parents

One of the most important factors in most people's (un)happiness is who their parents are. As you will learn in later chapters, up to 60 percent of our basic happiness or propensity to think happy thoughts may be genetically determined. Add to that the impact that parenting and childhood have on all of us, and it's easy to understand that luck in the 'parental lottery' is a fundamental component of many people's happiness. I deliberately use the word fundamental because parents, through DNA and actions, form the foundation on which you build your life, develop your mental models, and begin your work towards mastering the Mindchanging Model and disciplined thinking.

In my case, I can honestly say that I have had the most devoted and amazing parents I could ever wish for. Mom and Dad met in Solna, a working-class suburb of Stockholm, at a dance when she was 13 (claiming to be 15) and Dad was 16 (and to this day he feels the need to emphasize that no hanky-panky happened that night). What happened was that they fell in love as they floated across the dance floor and he whispered to her that she was "following him around like a postage stamp" (which completely confused mom, who spent days trying to decipher the compliment). Since then they have been a team. I've never heard them say a bad word to or about each other, or be grumpy, selfish, or lazy in their love. Instead, they have supported each other, stood by each other in adversity and joy, and been amazing parents to me and my older brother.

My father...

My father Lars was born in 1933 and grew up during the Second World War when Europe and the world was on fire. He also grew up in a poor home (they actually rented out the kitchen couch to a worker in their two-room apartment) and my grandfather went for long periods without a real job when, as a sailor, he saw the war put an end to his life at sea.

Dad became an elite athlete playing ice hockey in AIK Hockey in the Swedish National League, football in the Swedish top league, and also represented Sweden in bandy (an odd Swedish sport on ice). In his late teens, he became a certified plumber after an apprenticeship with my grandfather. It wasn't long before my father, a natural leader, began representing his much older colleagues in wage discussions and within the union, and later all the country's plumbers, then all workers, and then as a Social Democratic politician became Mayor of Stockholm (Swedish: borgarråd). His driving force was justice and the need for change in a labor market where workers worked six days a week, with few rights, significant work risks, and insecure pensions. He always found meaning and strength in his vision of a better society and in his opportunity, but also duty, to drive change. I could write endlessly about my wonderful father, but there is no room for that in this book.

In May 2017, he fell in the bathroom and became paralyzed

from the neck down, with only limited ability to connect with the muscles in his legs and arms. Since then, he has been confined to bed or a wheelchair and has been completely dependent on assistance to eat, go to the toilet, or scratch his chin. When he realized he was paralyzed, his first reaction was denial. You're wrong, just look at me, I'll walk again. He still has this deliberate delusion, and every now and then he can actually take a couple of steps when we take him to a hot pool. His second ambition was to set a new goal, one that he can work on every day: "I want to be the best patient possible." Since then, the book Lars Ahlvarsson has been created from his life and thoughts. He has become a dear friend and mentor to many assistants and hospital staff, traveled to Mykonos and Ibiza (most people have no idea how tough traveling as a paraplegic is and how much bruising and pain it involves), and most importantly, he has managed to stay positive and actually... happy.

This is for me one of the most important insights into how strong and true the underlying message of this book is: how you feel is based on how you talk to yourself, and it is possible to create happiness almost no matter how tough your situation is. For me, he is an endless source of inspiration and the counter-argument to anyone who claims that "what if you lose a leg" or other implied arguments against our ability to discipline or think to be happy. There is a theory that there are four types of happiness: one is the happiness when you look back on a happy life and feel joy about how you lived. Another type is the happiness derived from your position, your possessions, and your relative success; the third is derived from the 'now' and the physical and mental experiences of the 'now.' The last one is the happiness from living in harmony with your worldview, spirituality, and death. In my father's case, he is very proud and happy with the life he has lived. He is proud of his sons and grandchildren. He is proud of the career, the material conditions, of having surpassed his professional dreams and really made a difference. He is still madly in love with my mom. He loves sports and is glued (almost literally) to the sports channels, and he has made peace with death or what comes after and even opened the door to an afterlife after living a life as an ardent atheist. All this makes him happy, even though for him the present is now often terrible, painful, boring, and undignified.

My mom...

My mom is the opposite of my dad in many ways. While he has always been driven by duty and conviction, she has been driven by curiosity and a suppressed desire to see the world (most girls born in 1936 were naturally unable to travel and discover other countries during wartime and the post-World War II era). If Dad taught me how to excel on stage as a speaker or in negotiations, Mom honed my social skills, my curiosity to understand people, languages, and the world. Her dedication to her sons is in beautiful harmony with Dad's, and together they made a perfect team during my childhood and beyond.

Apart from her traveling adventures, Mom has always had a more pessimistic view of the unknown. Dad has always said yes and then tried to seize the opportunity; mom has belittled herself and more often seen what could go wrong rather than how much fun it would be if it went right. An example of this tendency to think worrying thoughts is how she has reacted to Dad being paralyzed and mostly hospitalized. She has become sadder and more depressed than he is, even though she is relatively healthy, has a loving family, and can have all the material comforts she wants. She feels sorry for Dad, and in her mind, she creates sad stories about his condition and worries about his happiness and future. I understand that this is the most common way of reacting to the situation that the love of your life and companion is paralyzed and hospitalized. However, for me, it highlights how differently people can think about a situation and that the experience of an event or situation is more important than the event or situation itself.

As a side note on how the wrong perspective can make you think thoughts that are very negative, I can tell you that my perfect childhood for a long time made me question whether I would ever have children myself because I could never be even half as good as my parents had been. I also questioned my relationships and was overly critical because I felt that those I was close to were not as loving and selflessly caring as my parents. So even a perfect childhood can create its negative truths.

Fortunately, I learned Mindchanging thinking, and as a result (and/or maybe it was "just" about finding the right girl), I had a beautiful marriage for ten years before we decided to go our separate ways as friends and, more importantly, a wonderful daughter who makes me be the best version of myself.

Now you know some of my family background and upbringing that has been instrumental in starting my Mindchanger journey. My professional career has been another major catalyst where I have started, developed, a few times crashed, and many more times succeeded and then sold companies. The entrepreneur's life, just like that of a kickboxer, is full of sweat, blood, and tears, and the passion and dedication required is similar (I wrote a book on the subject, Mission Possible, for the interested reader). To date, I have co-founded 24 companies, sold ten of them, crashed four (fortunately 20 years ago), and still own a portfolio of exciting businesses. I've been named a Global Leader of Tomorrow at the World Economic

Forum and have been listed as a thought leader in everything from the Wall Street Journal to Businessweek, Wired Magazine, and many more. I have advised organizations from Google to NATO, been given the Golden Keys to Miami by Mayor Levin, been awarded an honorary doctorate, and a host of other awards and recognitions (the interested reader can find more about me on Wikipedia or olaahlvarsson.com). I am not writing any of the above to impress or brag (this is important to explain to Swedish readers where bragging is a mortal sin, while American readers get excited and inspired by the successes of others). I am writing to make a more important point: I can thank the Mindchanging mindset and the way I talk to myself for all my successes, be it in sports or in business. A loving and respectful relationship with myself has been the basis for trying, often failing, but then trying again. Not thinking or feeling negativity has given me an excess of energy to explore, build, and develop in ways I couldn't even come close to before I started thinking in a disciplined way and found the tools to both feel and succeed better.

Dubrovnik 1997, World Kickboxing Championships, final 69kg

In summary

- Your parents and your upbringing play a big role in how you interpret the world and in your basic level of happiness, or what is called your Hedonistic Set Point, which is the level of happiness you are normally at and to which you gravitate regardless of whether bad or good things happen that temporarily affect your happiness.
- The first adult you choose as a role model often has a major impact on your life.
- Unexpected hobbies or phenomena can spark curiosity and accelerate learning, even for those who find school uninteresting.
- There is a big difference between actually getting in the ring and trying to follow your dreams and sitting in the audience and commenting.
- If you are good at talking to yourself and have a positive, friendly inner voice, it doesn't matter if you fail. It allows you to try again and again, and eventually you will succeed. This is often what success looks like in reality.

Thoughts to reflect on

- What chosen truths, positive and negative catalysts and thoughts have you inherited from your parents?
- What in your childhood characterizes you most now?
- How do you feel when you fail? Could you think about failure in a different way that feels better?
- Which non-parental adult did you look up to? Why, what qualities inspired you?

How the brain works and how you can make it work for you

THE BRAIN IS our most fascinating and powerful organ. While it accounts for only 2 percent of our body weight, it consumes a whopping 20 percent of our body's energy. Beneath your skull lies an intricate network of 16 billion neurons forming the cerebral cortex, followed by the cerebellum with another 70 billion cells - all interconnected to create everything you experience: what you see, feel, remember, know, and dream.

The very idea that our consciousness might not be part of an immortal soul or mysterious "self," but instead just cells firing synapses in a network, feels counterintuitive and wrong to most people. This feeling persists even as neurologists and researchers who study the latest findings struggle to accept "truths" in which consciousness and brain function are considered separate things. Whether you believe in such dualism can significantly impact your happiness and chosen truths, as we'll explore later.

Currently, the brain remains largely uncharted territory. Concepts like consciousness, dreams, and the interactions between different brain regions are still shrouded in mystery.

But recent years have witnessed remarkable breakthroughs in our understanding of the brain. One of the most important discoveries is brain plasticity - the brain's ability to be trained and developed throughout our lives. As neurologists would explain it: "Neural plasticity, also known as neuroplasticity or brain plasticity, can be defined as the ability of the nervous system to change its activity in response to intrinsic or extrinsic stimuli by reorganizing its structure, functions or connections." In simpler terms, your brain physically changes its wiring based on feedback.

This contradicts the previously common assumption that our brains reach peak development after adolescence with limited ability to change afterward. Instead, we now know that stimulating our brains causes continued development throughout our lives.

This is incredibly good news. It means that every time your brain is stimulated, it responds and evolves. This happens when you learn something new, whether it's riding a bike or using unfamiliar vocabulary. The brain that knows how to ride a bike is physically different from the brain that doesn't. While this doesn't mean anyone can become anything, it does mean we can program, reprogram, and develop our thinking. Anyone can, in principle, think virtually anything.

Think of your brain as a muscle that strengthens every time it recovers from a workout - the more you exercise, the stronger the muscle becomes. In fitness, the challenge isn't discovering how to lose weight or build muscle. Most people agree that eating healthy and exercising regularly eventually makes you fit. The same applies to mental fitness. The more you train your thinking - the way you talk to yourself - and the more positive catalysts you cultivate to support this process, the more mentally fit you become. Someone who feels sad, unhappy, angry, or jealous can change these states by becoming a skilled conductor of their inner voice, just as surely as going to the gym makes you stronger.

But just like getting your body in shape, developing a trained mind and disciplined thinking doesn't magically happen when you have an insight (or read a book). It takes practice. It's incredibly difficult to take command of your thoughts during a crisis, depression, or when overwhelmed by negative emotions. To continue the gym analogy, it would be like trying to lift more weight than ever before right after breaking your arm.

That's why it's important to continuously develop control over your inner voice by starting with simple challenges and gradually addressing more deeply rooted negative chosen truths - whether from years of being unkind to yourself, dwelling on negative experiences, or other factors fundamentally inhibiting your satisfaction with life.

'Chosen truths' aren't necessarily about describing actual events objectively. They're about your interpretation. If you felt lonely and unloved as a child because your parents were rarely around, that may be factually accurate - and truly sad. However, the truth you choose can be whether to blame yourself, believe you don't deserve love, blame your parents for your insecurities - or recognize that they probably did their best given their circumstances, knowledge and capacity, even if it wasn't enough. You can learn from their example what kind of parent you want to be for your own children.

Now that we understand we can train our brains, how does this work in practice? Studies show we think 80-90 percent of the same thoughts every day. If you reflect on this, you'll probably recognize the pattern. Each time you think a thought, you make it easier to think that same thought again because your brain already has the neural pathway established. It can quickly fire the right electrical impulses to repeat that thought, which is much easier than creating a new neural pathway for a new thought. This means if you're typically hard on yourself or frequently haunted by thoughts from past trauma, you'll likely continue thinking those familiar thoughts tomorrow - unless you actively take command of your thought patterns and build new pathways toward thoughts that make you feel better.

The brain naturally defaults to thinking the same thoughts it's thought before, so it takes real effort to replace a familiar thought with a new one. Try thinking: "I'm going to the kitchen to refill my coffee." Feels easy and natural, right? Now think instead: "I'm moving to Tokyo, changing my gender, and becoming a German teacher." For most people, the second thought feels complicated, requiring several seconds to process completely. Similarly, thoughts that challenge your self-image and destructive patterns can initially feel alien before becoming natural with practice.

Because changing thought patterns is usually a gradual process requiring time and effort. But it can also happen overnight, as when love turns to hate after discovering infidelity, or when fanatical Hitler Youth members who were ready to die for Hitler in 1945 couldn't relate to those feelings by 1946. As you've learned, the Mindchange model is based on the fact that how you talk to yourself determines how you feel. Knowing the brain is plastic allows you to program/train/coach it (choose whatever word feels right) to create more positive emotions and fewer negative ones.

Let's continue exploring how you can develop your understanding and thinking through deeper theory, concrete mental techniques, and different "maps" for designing a fulfilling life.

Growth mindset

One of my favorite TED Talks features Jo Boaler, a renowned mathematics educator and Stanford University professor, explaining how anyone can learn math when mindset becomes the key to faster, better learning. She's developed a method where students experience math through play, seeing mathematical concepts in songs, everyday objects, and by tackling seemingly impossible problems - making math exciting, beautiful, and inclusive.

Boaler's primary research focuses on developing mathematical mindsets. She argues that our beliefs about our ability to learn math significantly impact our success in the subject. She's written extensively about the importance of a 'growth mindset' in mathematics education, emphasizing that mathematical ability, even at advanced levels, can be developed by anyone through hard work and perseverance. She also highlights the harmful effects of a fixed mindset - the belief that our abilities are determined solely by innate talent.

Harvard Business Review describes a Growth Mindset this way: Individuals who believe their talents can be developed (through hard work, effective strategies, and input from others) have a growth-oriented mindset. They typically achieve more than those with a fixed mindset (those who believe their talents are innate gifts). This happens because they worry less about looking smart or failing and instead invest more energy in learning.

This principle applies at the organizational level too, where companies with a growth mindset typically outperform similar organizations with a fixed mindset.

This means that how you talk to yourself about your ability to learn directly affects that ability. Taking control of your inner dialogue through Mindchange thinking can enable both faster learning and better results.

Boaler also explores innovative learning approaches that activate more brain regions, combining sounds, conversations, varied environments, and different learning models that engage more of the brain than just the typically overloaded areas used for math problems. For children who begin hearing math in songs, seeing it in angles around their room, and engaging in ongoing mental math as they move through their day, mathematical learning accelerates exponentially.

Another inspiring example is Nadia Comaneci, the Romanian gymnast who won five Olympic gold medals and who, in 1976 at just 14 years old, earned the first perfect score of 10.0 in Olympic gymnastics history. Think about that for a moment - a 14-year-old performing flawlessly under immense pressure, despite fierce competition and the distracting camera flashes from journalists and spectators. I once had dinner with someone who trained alongside her, who shared what he believed was one of her key success factors: from a very young age, she believed she was destined to be a champion. She saw herself as special. She also trained like a champion - when other students did ten push-ups because the coach said to do ten, she did as many as she physically could. Her way of speaking to herself and creating her own story propelled her to gold medals and recognition as one of the century's greatest athletes across all sports. If you watch video of her perfect performance from Montreal, you can see her lips moving beforehand, telling herself she's the best and that "she can do this" - just before delivering the greatest gymnastics performance in history.

Our brain can kill and heal

Our brain is truly miraculous and mysterious. It loves stories and compelling narratives, often much more than facts or logical explanations. This explains why advertising works, why we love Hollywood movies, and why hero myths never go out of style. It's also why taking control of your inner dialogue is so powerful - you're essentially programming your brain's thoughts, feelings, and actions with words that become stories and ultimately create the narrative you live by, giving you a framework for understanding the world.

This is both frightening and encouraging. There are documented cases where thinking has caused death (as well as cases where not thinking has done the same). From the Indian patient who was among the first COVID cases and died from shock upon receiving the test results, to heart attacks triggered by fear when seeing a snake, to severe stress or other mental conditions. I've even heard accounts (though I haven't found conclusive evidence) of people falling toward certain death who actually die before impact. We don't need such extreme examples to recognize that the brain has enormous destructive potential - the power to make us feel bad, afraid, angry, jealous, vindictive, or utterly hopeless.

At the same time, substantial evidence shows that the brain can heal, and that positive, healthy thoughts not only promote overall wellbeing but lead to longer and arguably happier lives.

Stories are how marketers and brands seduce us consumers into buying their products, how startups create billion-dollar companies through vision and narrative, and how both democratic leaders and dictators attempt to control the agenda and attract followers to their worldview.

One of the most revealing examples of storytelling's power is the marketing campaign for Shreddies cereal. In their TV commercial, square Shreddies move along a conveyor belt under an inspector's watchful eye until one biscuit appears to be diamond-shaped (which is just the same square biscuit rotated 45 degrees). The next scene shows the manager angrily shouting: "Diamond shaped! Shreddies are supposed to be square... Have any of these gone out to consumers?" This is followed by an advertisement for "New Diamond Shaped Shreddies" - exactly the same product but with new packaging showing a model holding the "diamond shaped" biscuit. Sales increased significantly as consumers rushed to buy these "new" diamond-shaped cereal pieces. For a good laugh and visuals to accompany this story, I recommend Ogilvy & Mather's vice-president Rory Sutherland's

TED talk about the Shreddies diamond-shaped campaign.

What actually happened? Nothing changed about the product itself - it was the same cereal photographed from a different angle. But the entire experience and the consumer's feelings toward the brand changed because the story was fun and made the product feel new and likeable. The story became the value.

Just as advertising creates an essential component of value and experience, our inner stories create what we experience throughout our lives. This applies to stories like that of Jesus Christ (where for some, the story may be all there is) to whether a high school student tells herself she's beautiful or ugly as she gets ready for prom. That's why it's so crucial to take an honest look at the stories we choose to believe and that dominate our thinking. If you believe you have trauma that can never be healed, that you're always late because of ADHD and can't do anything about it, or that you're bad at math because your mom was - you're probably right. The same is often true for those who believe the opposite - they're also right, because the power of narrative can either limit or expand our potential for change.

When you truly understand that all our emotions arise from our brain and that the brain can be trained to make us feel better, perform better, and avoid destructive thinking, you'll also understand why Mindchange thinking is so important for living a happy, harmonious life. If you find this message repeated throughout the book, that's intentional. A story needs to be told, retold, and approached from different angles before it becomes the listener's or reader's story - one they fully understand, embrace, and use. Think about religion - most faiths encourage reading the same texts daily, reciting the same prayers, and maintaining the narrative through weekly gatherings, sometimes reinforced by warnings about the consequences of straying from the path.

Thank you, Professor Kahneman!

Daniel Kahneman, a psychology professor and Nobel laureate, discovered that we have two dominant thinking systems - a fast system that allows quick risk evaluation and decision-making, and a slow, more deliberate system.

The fast system looks for similarities: Is X like Y? When thinking fast, you search for familiar patterns. If you spot something dark that resembles a lion, you don't stop to wonder, "Is that a lion or perhaps a panther? Can I scratch behind its ears?" You run, because it looks like a lion. Those ancestors who didn't react this way didn't survive to become our ancestors.

Fast thinking has saved us as a species throughout history. It's excellent for quick decisions: If it looks like a lion, run! Most early humans lived in environments where slow thinkers died first. This fast-thinking system interprets what's happening before the slow system even engages.

The slow-thinking system examines what's most logical and reasonable. Rather than just identifying similarities, it calculates probabilities: How likely is it that X equals Y?

Imagine meeting a man in America who tells you he enjoys stories and organizing things. He's very methodical and somewhat shy. Asked whether he works in a library or as a pig farmer, most people guess librarian because he fits that profile. But if you think slowly and consider how many male librarians exist in America compared to men working in pig farming, there are far more pig farmers. So statistically, when meeting a random American man, he's more likely to be a pig farmer.

Here's another example: Do you think the world's most intelligent women marry men who are smarter or less smart than themselves? Many guess they marry equally intelligent or smarter partners. Of course they don't. They're smarter than almost everyone else in the world - statistically, they marry people who are less intelligent.

When thinking quickly, astrology often seems accurate and compelling. As an Aries, whenever I see my horoscope, it feels surprisingly on-target. If it really works, it seems intuitive - I always recognize traits or situations from my life. But thinking slowly, what's the likelihood that ancient Greeks watching stars and saying, "Hey Dimitris, that looks like a bear..." "Yeah, Stavros, and that looks like a little bear" could predict my life today, my future, or determine whether I should hire you or whether we're compatible for marriage? It seems highly improbable.

I'm eternally grateful to Professor Kahneman because after studying his work, I began double-checking my fast-thinking conclusions with more thoughtful, analytical slow thinking. This has saved me from both prejudice and poor decisions.

You're not so smart (and neither am I)

At this point, many astrology believers might object and want to debate. I'm not trying to argue whether astrology can predict the future or qualifies as real science. I'm simply noting that the probability seems extremely low to me - just as with claims that Jesus walked on water. The Mindchange model remains neutral to both claims and accommodates any chosen truth or belief system. It doesn't dictate whether you should be religious or believe in astrology. However, I am explaining some mechanisms driving our beliefs and chosen truths so you can examine your own assumptions with fresh eyes and perhaps discover ways to create stories that serve you better.

We carry many prejudices based on how we perceive things.

Consider the phenomenon of "priming." When we focus extensively on something, we become subconsciously primed to think about it. In one illustrative experiment, researchers divided participants into two groups for pre-lunch sessions. One group saw slow-moving animals, elderly people walking slowly, and experienced an overall sluggish workshop. The other group saw racing cars, running cheetahs, and had a fast-paced experience from beginning to end. When asked to walk to the lunch restaurant afterward, the "fast" group naturally walked much faster than the "slow" group, who moved at almost half the pace.

In his fascinating book "You're Not So Smart," author David McRaney explores the inaccuracies and biases we all carry. One phenomenon he highlights is that the beginning and end of an experience seem to matter more than what happens in between. If surgery is extremely painful at the beginning and end, it may feel more terrible than a much longer operation with less intense pain at those critical points, even though the latter objectively involved more total pain.

It's like relationships - you fall in love, have a great time, but the ending turns bitter, and you feel it was a bad relationship despite having perhaps ten wonderful years together. We all have these cognitive fallacies, and Mindchange thinking helps us recognize and address them from different angles. Kahneman doesn't suggest fast thinking is bad - he explains it's valuable to be able to think both quickly and slowly, and to view situations from multiple perspectives.

When thinking fast, statements like "real medicine doesn't come from a laboratory, it comes from nature" sound compelling, but are they accurate? Why do otherwise intelligent people believe that some miracle plant discovered in a remote tribal village might cure cancer when billions of dollars and brilliant scientists are collaborating worldwide with cutting-edge tools? It might be true, but what's the probability?

This same fast-thinking system that seeks patterns where none exist also makes us susceptible to conspiracy theories: We never went to the moon. The CIA destroyed the Twin Towers. Bill Gates created COVID to reduce the world's population.

These conspiracy theories emerge because we're too good at creating and believing stories. Research on people prone to conspiracy theories shows some common traits. They often lack power in their professional or personal lives, so they fill this void with powerful narratives where they alone possess knowledge that even major institutions haven't discovered - like aliens living at Area 51. This naturally makes life more exciting and creates a sense of significance.

Again, I'm not telling you whether to believe the Earth is round or flat. That's not my mission. My purpose is to help you understand that the stories you tell yourself create a dramatically different life experience and quality of life.

Are you threatened or curious?

Another model for understanding thinking describes different mental systems or states for handling various situations. These operate like programs or apps running in your brain. One such state is exploration - when we're in "explore" mode, we want to learn new things, have novel experiences, and look around corners. It feels exciting and stimulates curiosity. You welcome new people, like when someone brings an unexpected friend to dinner. You eagerly try unfamiliar foods. You want to explore - this is when humans function at their best.

But often, we operate in different states. On the ancient savannah, if a tiger appeared, your priorities instantly shifted.

In that situation, you weren't interested in meeting new people or trying exotic foods - you needed to run. You felt threatened. Your entire programming focused on survival: "How can I save myself?"

In modern life, this might manifest when you return home uncertain whether your partner still loves you or might break up with you. You feel threatened. In this state, you don't want to explore - you want to determine if there's a real threat. In a work scenario, if you fear being fired, you're unlikely to think, "Let's generate new ideas and invite more perspectives." Instead, you might say, "Why is she in this meeting? She's not part of our group" or "We've always done things this way - why change now? We've never tried this before."

Many readers will recognize these workplace reactions when colleagues (or even you) contract rather than expand, feeling threatened instead of embracing creative exploration. The theory suggests you can't move directly from "threatened" to "exploring." This is where I made numerous mistakes for years, both in relationships and professionally: "Come on, let's climb Mont Blanc! It'll be fun! Don't be so boring." For someone in a threatened state, such encouragement only increases their anxiety. Before they can explore, they need to reach a state of safety.

"Safe" is when you feel loved and secure, believing you're in it for the long haul. You can be yourself. In this state, you're comfortable sharing thoughts, accessing creativity and intelligence in work situations, and performing at your best - not just professionally but in relationships and life generally.

Fortunately, simple techniques can help people move from feeling threatened to feeling safe and curious. Physical touch, humor, and discussing long-term future plans top the list. Imagine your boss entering, giving you a friendly pat on the shoulder, then saying: "For next summer's kickoff in Chicago, I'd like you to lead that project because (making a joke) you're always the last one on the dance floor anyway - no one parties harder, so you might as well have it!" It's not particularly funny, but the combination of physical contact, future planning, and shared laughter creates safety, making it easier for you to contribute your best ideas.

This applies beyond work contexts to social situations and time with your children. I also use this model to examine my own thinking: Why am I reacting this way? Do I feel threatened? What would help me feel safe? If I feel safe, how might I explore this situation more creatively?

Situation, complication, solution

The situation-complication-solution model offers another powerful formula. The more polarized and contentious a situation becomes, the more important it is to guide the other person through a safe common starting point (the situation), making it easier to present a complication and solution. This approach aligns with how our brains process information: First, establish safety and confirm there's no immediate danger or conflict. Then understand the problem. Finally, hear a solution that resolves the issue.

When you start conversations by creating safety rather than immediately presenting problems, something transformative happens. This works particularly well with feedback or criticism. For instance, if someone says: "Don't leave your coffee cups all over the office," you immediately feel threatened and defensive. Your natural response might be: "I'm not the only one doing it" or "I have more important things to worry about."

If instead they began with: "I really enjoy working with you and we have so many exciting projects right now," and then added "but your coffee cups are everywhere," your reaction shifts completely. You think, "Oh, they are." Now you want to solve the problem because you feel safe. If they also suggest a solution - "Let's have a competition to see who's best at removing their cups" - you'll likely accept the constructive criticism and engage with the challenge.

One of history's most accomplished diplomats was Austrian prince Klemens von Metternich. He played crucial roles in defeating Napoleon, brokering peace, and designing the modern European balance of power system where multiple nations counterbalance any potentially dominant power. He also successfully negotiated with Emperor Napoleon himself. Metternich always opened these sessions by making Napoleon feel powerful and proud, acknowledging French superiority in various domains. These psychological techniques created the right mindset for every conversation, allowing Metternich to pursue his actual goals and address conflicts productively. If this approach worked with a dictator like Napoleon, it might work with your boss or partner too.

Summary

- The brain can be trained and developed throughout life.
- The brain loves storytelling.
- We easily embrace stories that create prejudices or implausible beliefs, making everything from magic to conspiracy theories compelling when we get seduced by the narrative.
- Stories can be so powerful they make us physically ill, but they can also make us healthier, braver, happier, and help us live longer.
- We have different pre-programmed psychological systems: one thinks fast and looks for similarities to quickly identify potential dangers; the other thinks slowly and examines the probability that something is actually true, often reaching different conclusions than our initial analysis.
- We also operate in different mental states: exploring, threatened, and safe. Our reactions vary dramatically depending on our current state of mind.
- By communicating using the situation-complication-solution formula, we can avoid unnecessary conflicts and polarization because the person we're communicating with doesn't feel threatened.
- You can learn to stop negative thoughts and create positive ones, but this shift requires active practice and time (though sometimes it can happen instantaneously).

Thoughts to reflect on

- Practice seeing a situation or phenomenon quickly first, then reaching a more thoughtful conclusion. What do you think of hip hop? Or: can you judge a book by its cover?
- What prejudices and fixed ideas do you hold about things you actually know very little about?
- Choose a firmly rooted belief you hold. Then try thinking thoughts that challenge or overturn that belief.
- Try drafting an email to a colleague who never speaks up in meetings or contributes to discussions. Use the situation-complication-solution model.
- Apply the same model to tell your partner you want them to be more romantic.

What is a consciousness?

BY NOW YOU understand that the brain is plastic, loves stories, and that these stories can dramatically affect how we feel both physically and mentally. But what about the soul or our consciousness? The riddle of consciousness remains largely unsolved, with the answer heavily depending on who you ask and what philosophy or religion underpins their view (or how they talk to themselves, if you prefer). Let me summarize some recent scientific findings and important philosophical and religious perspectives on consciousness.

If you ask a neuroscientist...

Based on recent findings, most scientists agree that what we perceive as consciousness and our sense of "self" are essentially electrical impulses in our brains. This conclusion comes from advanced scanning technologies like PET scans and fMRI, which allow scientists to "listen in" on brain activity and explore its mysteries. This contradicts our intuitive experience of a "self" - it feels strange to imagine that love, hope, fear, humor, and all the other qualities that make being human so beautiful are merely electrical impulses between brain cells.

According to neuroscientist Pontus Wasling, "there are few other examples where the difference between what science says and what we humans think is so great." Recent developments in AI have interesting implications here. The sophisticated reasoning capabilities of systems like ChatGPT suggest that neurons and related physical elements (like hormones and neurotransmitters) might be sufficient to explain consciousness, without needing other constructs or a soul.

This scientific shift parallels how Christianity had to abandon the literal view that paradise and "heaven" were physically above the clouds once airplanes crossed the sky without encountering angels. Personally, I align with the scientific perspective and have no problem with this view. I understand why many people resist the idea that individually "dumb" cells could, when connected, create the intelligent consciousness that put humans on the moon and created our most beautiful art and literature.

Remember that Mindchange thinking doesn't dictate what to believe, but offers a framework to control how you think about what you believe and how it affects your wellbeing. If you're comfortable believing you have an eternal soul separate from your "flesh bag" body, that's a perfectly acceptable chosen truth. If instead you fear your soul might go to hell for your sins, the Mindchange model allows you to reprogram that belief and choose a different truth.

Returning to the scientific understanding of consciousness, researchers have localized it to specific brain regions and learned something about the processes of thinking and feeling, but haven't yet discovered exactly how consciousness and the perception of life emerge. We're fairly certain consciousness ceases when the brain stops firing signals between cells, and when patients are brain-dead or in persistent vegetative states. Puzzlingly, some supposedly brain-dead or non-conscious people have regained consciousness after being awake without awareness, making consciousness even more mysterious.

A prevailing scientific theory suggests consciousness evolved as a trait that helps us live in larger social groups and better communicate with and understand others. One fascinating hypothesis involves REM sleep, which we all experience nightly. Sleep begins with deep sleep where we organize and store the day's impressions and memories. The Uber driver's license plate you no longer need to remember gets filed away, while your morning meeting stays top of mind. After about 90 minutes of deep sleep, we transition to REM sleep, and this cycle repeats with longer REM periods throughout the night.

During REM sleep, our eyes move rapidly beneath closed lids while the brain toggles various "switches" on and off, recalibrating for tomorrow's experiences. We're temporarily paralyzed to prevent acting out our dreams and potentially harming ourselves or bedmates. In this state, we experience the most bizarre dreams as random neural switches activate and deactivate simultaneously. (Don't feel guilty about dream content - it's beyond your control. I once dreamed Saddam Hussein and I were ritually killing Jesus!)

The theory suggests that when our ancestors descended from trees millions of years ago, they developed REM sleep because they could do so without falling from branches. As connections between brain cells create new memories and experiences during dreams, our brains develop and reprogram. This means you literally have a slightly different brain every morning. It's like sleepwalking for an hour and exercising while you sleep, waking up more alert. Throughout evolution, we developed the neocortex - the "new" brain region housing abstract thinking, emotions, and reasoning. As our brains formed more synapses, this fueled more REM sleep and thinking, which further developed our brains, until our ancestors left Neanderthals far behind.

Not everything happens in our conscious brain, though. Many processes beyond basics like breathing and nervous system regulation work better when we don't overthink them and instead use what's called the subconscious. It's often said that the greatest poetry emerges from the shadowy realms of consciousness. I've experienced this firsthand in the fighting ring. The worst thing that can happen is suddenly becoming too conscious and having to deliberately decide every move instead of achieving flow and letting my subconscious skills - developed through decades of training - work their magic.

Materialists ...

Can electrical stimulation in a laboratory create the illusion of a soul? In experiments, stimulating certain brain regions has induced feelings of being part of an interconnected universe and a cosmic community. Similar experiences are reported by those who've used psychedelic drugs. Another common phenomenon in both contexts is the sensation of leaving one's body and looking down on it. Experiments show that we can shift our perception from our bodies to other objects, like a fake hand or even another body.

A fun demonstration is the rubber hand experiment (Google "Rubber Hand Experiment"), where a researcher places a screen between a subject's real arm and a fake arm positioned as if it were their own. The researcher then strokes both the real and fake arms until the subject's perception shifts to feeling sensations in the fake arm. Suddenly, the researcher produces a hammer and strikes the fake hand - and the subject reacts as if their real hand were hit. Similar experiments using cameras can shift your sensory experience to an image of yourself projected in front of you, essentially relocating your consciousness outside your actual body.

This doesn't have to be depressing or reduce our sense of wonder if there's no divine soul or true self separate from the brain's electrical impulses. I find it magical - it means we can embark on a lifelong journey exploring the brain's complex beauty on our path to greater happiness and fulfillment. All the answers are in your own brain, without needing stars, magical beings, fate, or traumas stored in your cells. It's frightening but exhilarating.

The being or non-being of the soul depends on who you ask

According to Christianity and most other religions, the idea that everything boils down to neurons and biology oversimplifies God's creation. Instead, they posit a material body and non-material soul. The body returns to ashes and dust at death, while the soul's fate depends on how good a Christian you've been. Sinners face hell on judgment day while the faithful enjoy heavenly glory.

Similar narratives appear in most religions, where the soul or consciousness exists alongside the material body and continues after death through reincarnation, heaven, hell, Valhalla, or Nirvana.

If you asked a "burner" instead (participants in Burning Man, the transformative social experiment in Nevada's desert where 80,000 people live without money, using kindness and inclusion as currency), they and millions worldwide with similar views would say they're spiritual rather than religious. They might explain the soul as part of an interconnected universe that guides us to exactly where we need to be, with everything happening for a reason.

Many in the burner community believe consciousness is interconnected and accessible through psychedelic substances like psilocybin mushrooms, ayahuasca, DMT, LSD, peyote, and other mind-altering compounds. Views on these experiences typically split two ways: the materialist perspective sees the resulting images and experiences as products of the individual's expanded consciousness, offering new perspectives on themselves and reality. The more mystical view holds that the spirit animal encountered during an ayahuasca journey or the fractals seen on LSD are actually real, connected to external magical forces with genuine meaning accessed through the drug experience.

Within this growing community, there's a fluid belief in something greater - energies, frequencies, dimensions, numerical patterns, or astrological forces governing our thinking and being. The common thread is that we originate from stars and will exist forever as our immortal atoms transform until the end of time.

This revival of 1960s New Age hippie philosophies is spreading, especially among adults who had religious upbringings but abandoned their faith and now fill that existential void with increasingly magical explanations of consciousness and the universe. I'm not sure if leaving religious faith universally creates a void needing to be filled, or why magical thinking feels so appealing, but there's no doubt many people believe in forces beyond physical explanations or scientific understanding.

This is particularly evident in the hyper-individualistic, success-worshipping United States, where many come from religious backgrounds, have left childhood faith behind, but as adults struggle with being just collections of atoms that briefly exist in an infinite universe. This is especially prevalent among those who've achieved career and social success but still feel something missing and seek something more meaningful.

How we mature and become more aware (or not)

We've all experienced the frustration of trying to reason with a child too young to understand or follow advice. Equally frustrating is dealing with an adult too stubborn or immature to grasp rational arguments. On a larger scale, we see this in subcultures like gangs or militant activists with their own rules and meaning-making systems, or even in national phenomena like America's gun obsession or British football hooliganism that mystify much of the world. Why do we see reality so differently? One reason may be that we operate at different maturity stages with different hierarchies of needs.

Abraham Maslow was an American psychologist renowned for his hierarchy of needs theory, which states that what we prioritize depends on our position in a needs hierarchy, with lower needs like food and safety requiring fulfillment before we can develop thinking and pursue social or self-actualizing goals.

He argued that human needs follow a hierarchical structure where lower levels must be satisfied before higher levels:

- Physiological needs: Basic survival requirements like food, water, air, shelter and sleep.
- Security needs: Once physiological needs are met, we seek safety and security, including physical safety, financial security and stability.
- Love and belonging needs: With security established, we pursue social connection and relationships, including friendship, family and romantic partnerships.
- Self-esteem needs: When love and belonging needs are satisfied, we seek self-esteem, respect, recognition and achievement.
- Self-actualization needs: The highest level involves achieving our full potential, pursuing personal development and reaching contentment.

According to Maslow, we're motivated to fulfill needs in this hierarchical order, starting with physiological needs and progressing upward. If lower needs remain unmet, we lack motivation for higher needs. The theory suggests motivation shifts from external factors to internal drivers like personal development and self-actualization as we ascend the hierarchy. Maslow's framework helps explain individual behavior and applies to larger groups and organizations.

A modern counterpart to Maslow is Professor Robert Kegan, a psychologist who developed a theory of adult development describing how individuals mature through different life stages. Kegan's theory recognizes that people continuously evolve, with each developmental stage presenting new challenges and growth opportunities. At these stages, we understand the world in fundamentally different ways.

Kegan identifies five adult development stages, each characterized by distinct thinking, reasoning and world-understanding approaches. This focuses on adult development rather than childhood development, though child development provides a useful metaphor.

These stages are:

- The impulsive stage: Typical of young children, characterized by immediate gratification of needs and desires. Adults at this stage show poor impulse control, prioritize themselves and their needs, and make short-sighted choices without considering consequences.
- The imperial stage: Common among teenagers and young adults, marked by social comparisons, identity formation, and desire for recognition. Many adults remain here, continuously comparing themselves to neighbors, social media influencers, or colleagues. Their self-worth

and priorities depend on others' opinions or perceived opinions.

- Interpersonal stage: Typical of early adulthood, featuring increased awareness of others' perspectives and needs, relationship focus, and developing empathy and interpersonal skills. At this stage, people seek to understand others and themselves more deeply, driven by development rather than comparison.
- Institutional stage: Common in middle age, characterized by abstract and analytical thinking, understanding complex systems and institutions, and navigating social and organizational structures. This stage recognizes society's interconnectedness and that simple truths can't encompass reality's complexity.
- Inter-individual stage: Rare and achieved by a small percentage of people. It features deep self and other understanding, capacity for self-reflection and introspection, and ability to tolerate ambiguity and complexity. Here, seemingly opposing thoughts and opinions can coexist. One understands the world through interacting systems of systems - complex patterns of factors interacting with other systems - gaining deeper understanding.

According to Kegan, we progress through these stages throughout our lives, each building on the previous one. However, not everyone reaches the higher development stages, and some remain in earlier stages.

Kegan's theory significantly impacts personal development, leadership development, and organizational change. Understanding these developmental stages helps individuals and organizations better support growth, both personally and in dealing with others who have different meaning-making frameworks.

It also profoundly affects our internal dialogue. From an egocentric worldview, through a normative worldview based on group norms, to a much more complex perspective encompassing seemingly contradictory viewpoints simultaneously.

In our increasingly complex world, developing more sophisticated models to understand reality becomes crucial, often requiring us to embrace apparently opposing viewpoints. For example, I might hate Satanists generally but enjoy a hard rock band with Satanic themes because I like their music. I might despise Arsenal as a Liverpool fan, considering them barely human, while recognizing that without Arsenal, I'd lose my favorite football experience - playing against them. As we mature, we embrace complexity and realize we can hold different, even contradictory thoughts simultaneously. I love my wife and don't want anyone else, yet I notice an attractive woman passing by. I love my kids while finding them occasionally annoying.

In Kegan's higher maturity levels, we see the world differently than at lower stages - viewing it as interacting systems of systems rather than us-versus-them. However, Kegan observes that people at lower maturity levels cannot understand higher-level thinking. Imagine the ultra-capitalist, egotistical character from "Wolf of Wall Street" meeting someone deeply committed to sustainability. After a press conference, alone together, he might say: "Come on, we're alone now. Drop the green bullshit. Where's the money in this? You're holding out! Let's get some escorts. You know you want to." He fundamentally cannot comprehend how someone at a higher development level thinks.

Why does this matter? Most of the world's dictators and totalitarian leaders remain stuck in early Kegan stages, locked in polarizing conflicts with other groups, countries, and individuals rather than seeing the world holistically. Hitler scapegoated Jews, using us-versus-them as his foundation, and categorized people as superhumans or subhumans. I believe the world needs the opposite - a completely different narrative that embraces complexity and unites people.

It starts with how you lead yourself and then how you lead others. As Kegan explains, our values shift through developmental stages. At the third level, where others' perspectives become important, we have tribal thinking - the street gang ready to kill for their norms and values. Similarly, countries oppose each other, as do religions.

That's why I believe we need a consciousness revolution where we find commonalities at higher complexity and maturity levels, developing systems that accommodate other people's systems from this foundation.

Summary

- Neurologists view 'consciousness' as electrical impulses in the brain, with emotions and thoughts as responses to neurotransmitter stimuli. Scientific evidence hasn't confirmed a 'soul' or consciousness separate from the body.
- It feels like we have a "self" and consciousness separate from bodily functions. Most religions see the soul as something greater than our current physical body.
- How you view consciousness, mind, brain, and their relationships affects how you talk to yourself.
- We mature along a developmental ladder where different needs become important at certain stages. Understanding these development stages helps you better understand yourself and others.

Thoughts to reflect on

Where do you see yourself on Maslow's ladder? Are you focused primarily on survival or material standards, being part of the right group, being important within that group, or fulfilling your deepest dreams and self-realization?

Where would you place yourself on Kegan's scale? Do you care greatly about others' opinions, or have you developed your own perspective (be honest)? Do you think mainly in us-versus-them terms?

A story to help you remember the main message of the chapter:

> Imagine four friends who all use Instagram extensively but for completely different reasons and in different ways. One doesn't care about others' opinions and proudly claims "I don't give a shit what people think." This person aggressively messages unknown profiles, indifferent to rejection. They post poorly considered pictures and misinformation without awareness of how others perceive them. The second friend wants maximum followers and likes, therefore pretending to appreciate major influencers and sometimes directly requesting likes when not too embarrassing. They occasionally feel depressed or stressed seeing others' apparently perfect lives and appearances. They might post significantly older photos and use filters to enhance their appearance. Many posts reflect what's considered "correct" thinking - from environmental commitments to political positions - but without genuine commitment. The third friend doesn't particularly care about Instagram but uses it mainly to connect with others on similar inner journeys. They rarely post except from yoga retreats, sound healing ceremonies, or other transformative events.

Extended digital detox periods sometimes give way to posts shared to benefit others rather than for selfish reasons. The fourth friend recognizes social media as an important channel for driving opinion and change, wanting to leverage their presence to gather and engage important networks for positive impact. Whether certain aspects are superficial or silly matters less than channeling engagement toward issues affecting everyone. These users have dramatically different priorities in life. Can you identify which Kegan developmental stages they represent?

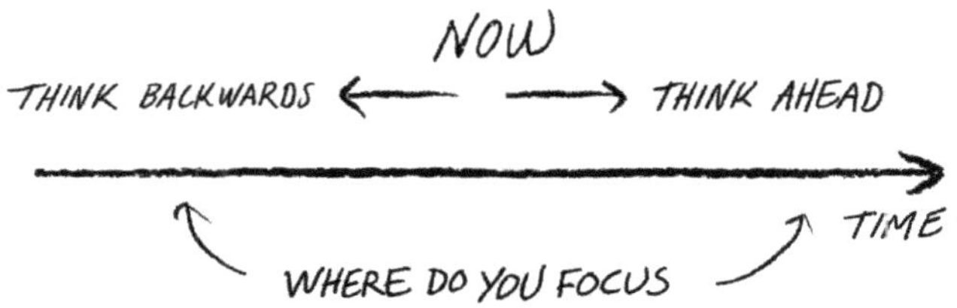

Popular stories (And why?)

"In life, you have to choose to plant good or bad seeds in your subconscious."

- Vex King, Good Vibes Good Life

AS MENTIONED EARLIER, our brains love stories. This is true for everyone, though some people are more story-driven than others, and as you'll see, some cultures are also more story-oriented. In his brilliant book Fantasyland, Kurt Andersen explains why the United States has an overdose of stories ever since the ultra-religious, free-thinking, and magic-believing first settlers became excited by the narrative of a new promised land, a land under God, and boarded ships to America. For them, one of the new nation's cornerstones was the freedom to believe in anything. Moreover, they were adventurers and risk-takers (would you take your children on a wooden ship to an unknown land where dangerous "savages" roamed?). This gene pool of individualistic, history-loving, somewhat naive settlers created a culture based on stories, from being God's hand-picked people to the home of the brave and many other powerful tales.

Andersen argues that since the 17th century, this has led to everything from witch trials to more religious sects and new churches than anywhere else, making America the only highly religious nation among top economies where most people believe in the Second Coming of Christ, Armageddon, and astrology. In business, these same characteristics created the advertising industry whose primary mission is telling (exaggerated, favorable) stories to seduce consumers. But these genes also created Hollywood, with its film star ideals and stories that touch and inspire billions worldwide.

Hollywood also has a knack for dramatizing real events and inventing horror stories that inspire real-life atrocities in a wave-like escalation of violence (consider how harmless the first Frankenstein film with Boris Karloff seems compared to The Texas Chainsaw Massacre or The Terminator). Andersen argues that the irresistible pull to create and believe in stories has generated countless fictions throughout American history - from secret societies like the Illuminati supposedly ruling the world or possessing magical Holy Grails, to believing Native Americans worked for the devil and Christians had a duty to kill them, to the Communist scare, the 1960s hippie movement, and more recent phenomena like Dungeons & Dragons, Scientology, or crystal healing, the Metaverse, social media, augmented reality, or the belief we're living in a simulation. In short, Americans particularly enjoy good stories and want to believe things that feel right and exciting, even without solid evidence.

Because the US excels at both creating new technologies and telling stories, we're all now bombarded with these innovations and narratives, changing societal structures and the inner dialogues of listeners/viewers/members/players/victims worldwide.

Why do we love stories so much? Beyond entertainment, campfire stories traditionally passed culture from leaders to younger generations. Religious rituals were performed through stories. Stories helped collective groups build and strengthen community, sharing origins, values, dreams, and what mattered most. For people of the past, stories offered the only glimpse of distant places or lives different from their tribe or monotonous farm existence. Later, artists could describe great battles in faraway lands, while theater performances made audiences gasp as special effects created roaring lions or firing cannons. This escapism is probably essential to being human, from children's role-play and drawing to pretentious artists doing similar things with bigger budgets. In historical times, stories were collective and primarily religious, creating God-fearing, hardworking serfs or nationalistic young men willing to kill and die for God and King.

Today's stories differ in several important ways: they're more individualistic or clustered around subcultures and interests. They reach us at unprecedented scale, speed, and quality, creating an exponentially growing sea of content. The danger is that individuals must navigate this ocean and understand how stories affect them both consciously and subconsciously. To feel safe, many crave belonging and protection from like-minded tribes, filling fan clubs, street gangs, political parties, and Burning Man gatherings with members wanting to share and expand their narratives with similar people.

The stories you choose to believe and embrace are important ingredients in your inner story, essentially creating your "default setting" for internal dialogue. By default, I mean your starting point shaped by DNA, experiences, where and when you grew up, your culture, and all other factors making you think, feel, and react as you do. From this baseline, you can begin your Mindchange journey. For example, discussing Darwin and evolution is more challenging with someone raised in a Pentecostal community who was homeschooled by a teacher insisting every Bible word is literally true (even Jonah living inside a whale until promising God to make amends) than with a secularized Swede.

Popular stories (and why?)

ARE THERE COMMON themes in the stories we want to hear and believe? Curiously, literature contains recurring stories. The hero's journey appears in many historical works. Today, we have popular narratives like Star Wars, where young Luke is whisked from his dull life by the mysterious Jedi wizard Obi-Wan for an important mission to Tatooine, only to embark on saving the universe from evil. This mirrors Harry Potter being taken by wizard Dumbledore for adventures at Hogwarts, only to discover he's the chosen one who must save the world from evil Voldemort. Or consider young Hobbit Frodo, led by wizard Gandalf from his quiet, somewhat boring Shire life to take the ring to Rivendell, until he too becomes the chosen one saving the universe.

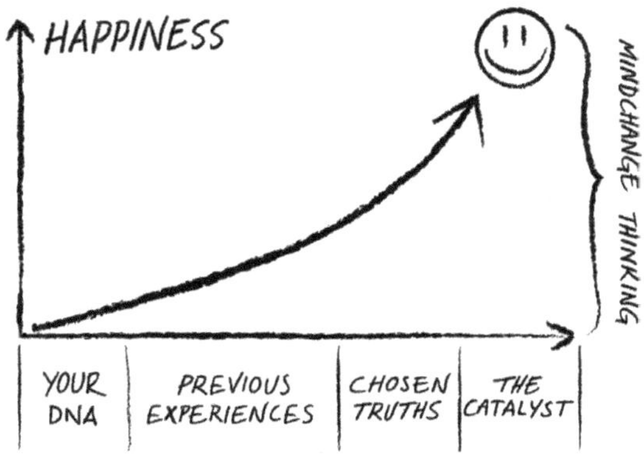

Simultaneously, we want to feel special (who doesn't?). Stories positioning us as chosen by Jesus, among the few understanding global conspiracies, or in an army doing Allah's work make us feel important - much more significant than being mere atoms in an infinitely vast universe. Strong narratives of success, beauty, and achievement in our global media society, where we constantly see others' successes worldwide, unfortunately lead many to compare themselves unfavorably, feeling ugly, poor, bored with their lives, hating their jobs, and believing they've been given a raw deal.

Only when you realize you're the writer and producer of your own stories can you learn, step by step, to take command of these narratives and create stories making you happier. This won't happen overnight, but eventually, thought by thought, your new stories will replace old ones.

In the following section, we'll examine different starting points for internal narrative before exploring how to become truly self-authoring.

Freud or Valhalla, take your pick

We're probably the only species aware of our inevitable death. To cope with thoughts of mortality, humans have always sought belief systems making death less frightening or even desirable. Religions commonly help people find meaning during life but can also offer rewards after death. Suicide bombers, Vikings, and martyrs across religions willingly sacrifice their lives, knowing they'll experience happiness afterward.

Philosophy has struggled with life's meaning since time immemorial, creating countless schools of thought. How we make sense of things and what we hold true plays a major role in societal development. What begins as philosophical discussion among learned people in tea rooms becomes revolution when translated into politics. This applies to humanistic approaches creating Western liberal societies centered on individuals, or to collectivism as in Sparta or communist states subordinating individuals to the collective. Marx's philosophy became the Soviet Union and Mao's China, while Nietzsche's ideas were distorted to support fascism and Nazi Germany. That's why a society's basic philosophy and moral foundations are critically important. For individuals, how you interpret and understand the world forms a central part of your basic attitude. For both society and individuals, lacking a basic narrative creates insecurity.

Understanding that differences in chosen truths form the foundations of different societies helps explain polarization and why individuals in different cultures react fundamentally differently to the same events.

Philosophy is often criticized as an elite academic club discussing old theoretical problems with little value for humanity or societal development. However, philosophy often initiates snowballs that trigger event chains. Philosophy establishing human equality led to abolishing slavery. Discussions among French intellectuals sparked the French Revolution and influenced the US Constitution.

Your worldview dictates your inner voice

What you believe and your life philosophy and spirituality are, as mentioned earlier, key ingredients determining your internal dialogue, how you understand the world, and what thoughts and actions you pursue. This applies to religious beliefs as well, so I've reflected on common thought systems and religions below to show how they fit the Mindchange model and how your beliefs determine your worldview and inner dialogue. This section is not essential reading for starting to apply mindchange thinking but is an important backdrop for the interested reader that wants a deeper understanding. I have therefore made the section Italic so that the less interested reader can skip to the next chapter on Happiness.

Political beliefs

A strong connection exists between how we understand the world and how societies form. This makes the ability to think consciously and become self-actualizing so important as a global competence.

Below are examples of how ideas become philosophies and then political systems shaping societies.

The communist worldview centers on inherent struggle between capitalists and workers or proletariat, with inevitable revolution where workers take over production means to own them jointly. Individual freedom to conduct business or generate profits is exchanged for a state caring for everyone according to their needs and drawing from everyone according to their abilities.

As a committed communist, you believe world inequalities stem from economic injustice and capitalists stealing wealth rightfully belonging to workers. Where communism has been attempted, it has produced large-scale experiments with well-documented disastrous results in the Soviet Union and Mao's China. In some micro-communities like hippie collectives, kibbutzim, or employee-owned tech startups, communal models have worked better than pure capitalism.

As a Nazi (or other fascist believer), you reject human equality. Instead, you believe in Übermensch and Untermensch, superior and inferior races or bloodlines. In these societies, democracy and immigration (except for exploitable labor) weaken upper castes. The belief that the smartest, strongest, and most powerful should rule has been the historical norm in almost all empires and societies. Since the French Revolution and American independence, despotic fascist rulers have declined. However, "strongmen" leaders are surging in countries like Turkey, the Philippines, Hungary, Trump's America, and Putin's Russia.

In the Western liberal tradition I grew up with, all people having equal value and rights is undeniable fact. For us, individual free choice and rights to pursue happiness and prosperity are fundamental. A generally positive attitude toward international cooperation to avoid sub-optimization and increase universal prosperity has been the underlying assumption for many. This has changed dramatically over the past two decades, as voices against globalization, immigration, international cooperation, and other once-shared views face siege. In Trump's worldview, America must come first, even if allies and enemies receive unfair shares. According to Trump, crooked leftists have corrupted America, and only by following him (not the "fake news" media) will America become great again. This mix of patriotism and promises of prosperity and pride from the "good old days" resonates strongly with those who haven't experienced global economy benefits and groups who have declined in both professional and personal value. Add social media, alternative media, fake news, and foreign powers manipulating social platforms, and we face perhaps the greatest threat to democracy since the Berlin Wall fell.

Your political landscape view affects your lens for evaluating people and events. As polarization increases, it becomes harder to avoid choosing sides between Republicans and Democrats, America and China, Russia and NATO, or mask-wearing versus no masks during COVID. Mindchange thinking doesn't argue for one view over another. Even seemingly fundamental principles like human rights aren't given or "natural states." For tens of thousands of years, human rights weren't the norm but rather the opposite: tribalism, slavery, bloody conquests, and disregard for human dignity. What Mindchange does is challenge you to examine your chosen political views and consider how they affect your internal dialogue. As a mental exercise, try adopting the opposite view and see where it takes your inner voice.

Religious belief systems

I believe humans are programmed to develop religious beliefs, just as we crave stories. Like our needs for love, friendship, and family, we seem to need greater stories or meaning.

When Stalin tried abolishing religion in Russia, creating totalitarian militant atheism, Orthodox Christians and Muslim Caucasians continued believing and practicing underground, despite potential punishment and career limitations. Stalin also failed to abolish the Russian Santa Claus, which instead became incorporated into Soviet narrative.

Why do we believe in God(s)? One reason supported by billions is that God actually exists. With this worldview, earthly life becomes a passage and test for a different, more exciting afterlife.

Another reason we believe is that the very idea of being tiny organisms in a vast, cold, deterministic universe governed by physics laws is somewhat frightening and demeaning.

Christianity really nailed it

I'm impressed by Christianity's historical role and resilience as an organization. Founded in the first century AD, the Vatican remains one of the world's most powerful institutions with 1.3 billion baptized Catholics, making it humanity's most widespread faith.

The Church teaches that every spiritual soul is created immediately by God, not "produced" by parents, and is immortal: it doesn't perish when separated from the body at death and will reunite with the body at final resurrection.

For a Christian, "talking to yourself and creating an inner dialogue that makes you happier" can mean embracing the notion that the inner conversation is God's divine version of you and your consciousness. Within Christianity lies a clear path to good life, and I would argue that Christianity, along with other major religions, has been among history's most important catalysts for happiness and meaning (regardless of whether God exists).

Christianity has one important difference from Islam: the Bible was written by humans, mostly long after Jesus supposedly lived. It's therefore easy to accept different interpretations and even human mistakes or misunderstandings when reading the Bible. The Quran, however, is considered written by God through Prophet Muhammad's hands, making reading the Quran more like talking directly to Jesus than reading the Bible, in the sense that contradicting the text is more difficult. From a Mindchange perspective, your religious beliefs influence many other choices, thoughts, and feelings, making them important components of your core beliefs. For example, believing in an afterlife that will be wonderful might make you less afraid of death than someone without afterlife beliefs.

Buddhism is about not talking to yourself

For Buddha, all suffering comes from ego or self. As mentioned earlier, we spend half our waking hours talking to ourselves through internal dialogue. According to Buddhism, eliminating ego is the highest goal and only path to Nirvana. In Buddha's teachings, consciousness is illusion resulting from wrong thinking (i.e., talking to yourself incorrectly). The enlightenment path is meditation. To summarize his advice: stop thinking, start meditating.

To explore Buddha's views on Mindchange thinking, I uploaded Buddha's teachings to an AI chatbot and interviewed him in this book's appendix. He offers interesting perspectives on everything from life's meaning to whether I should attempt another kickboxing comeback.

Islam

Islam is one of history's most important thought schools, defining meaning maps for almost 2 billion people.

In Islam, there are good things (halal) and bad things (haram). Your afterlife existence depends on the relationship between halal and haram.

When Muslims sleep, they touch God's kingdom where their soul goes after death when the body separates into dust and the soul faces judgment.

According to renowned Muslim scholar Nasar Mannan, sleep in Islam mirrors death's state.

Souls experience death just as bodies do. But the Qur'an reveals that God's chosen ones' souls are recalled from death after varying periods - some after three days, some after a week, others after 40 days. Their new life brings extreme bliss, sweetness, and enjoyment. Righteous servants strive in complete devotion to attain this life, exerting themselves maximally to rid themselves of worldly life impurities.

This shifts focus from earthly life to the truly important blissful afterlife.

For Muslims, the inner dialogue for happy living should align with divine will to live according to the Holy Quran and serve God.

Hinduism

Hinduism is India's ancient religion representing about 15 percent of world population. It isn't a single unified religion and has no founder, single teacher, or prophets. Hindus believe in a universal soul or god called Brahman, worshipped in many different forms. These forms include complementary attributes of male and female deities in both human and animal forms. Hindu sects may worship their own divinities, but these are simply different approaches to God. Brahman is often represented in threefold form: Brahman as universe creator, Vishnu as preserver, and Shiva as destroyer.

Hindus believe the soul is immortal and upon bodily death transforms into new earthly life. Whether this life improves or worsens depends on how much good or evil occurred in the previous life - the law of karma. A series of good lives breaks this cycle, leading to final soul absorption into Brahman.

A good internal narrative for Hindus should include living righteously because future higher incarnation depends on this.

Atheism and secular humanism

A much smaller group consists of atheists who believe divinity doesn't exist and all gods are human-made fictions. Globally, 500-800 million people identify as atheists, with another equally large group claiming no religious belief, and yet another group leaving the door open to something beyond us.

The strongest argument for atheism and secular humanism is that no scientific reasons support belief in Christianity, Islam, or other religions. For believers, personal experience and God's ability to transcend scientific understanding by being a superior being beyond human comprehension provides sufficient evidence.

According to their own definitions: Secular humanists are non-religious people striving to live fulfilling, meaningful, ethical lives using reason and empathy to guide decisions and actions.

Secular Humanists base their worldview on reason and science, rejecting supernatural or divine beliefs.

For secular humanism, death means game over, so their personal narrative demands meaning, happiness, and fulfillment in this life, unlike many religious beliefs where earthly existence merely qualifies one for a more wonderful afterlife.

Astrology

Religious beliefs aside, approximately 30 percent of American adults believe in astrology, with an overwhelming proportion being women. This ranges from finding it entertaining to see what stars or tarot cards predict, to genuinely believing zodiac signs determine who we are and life events as a real science (which it isn't - in fact, it's the most common example of pseudoscience, defined by Oxford Dictionary as: a collection of beliefs or practices falsely considered based on scientific method).

Having a belief or even intentional delusion can be beautiful and a happiness source. But when astrology is used to categorize people professionally, as in "I work better with Aries but can't stand working with Leos," it becomes problematic (and illegal discrimination in most civilized countries). If you replaced zodiac signs with different races - "I work well with blacks but can't stand working with whites" - most people would recognize it as non-inclusive and unfair.

Ancient religions and ancient wisdom

Ancient religions share commonalities in organizing everything into good and evil systems. Ancient Greeks had warring titans and gods, while in Norse mythology Odin, Thor, Freyr, and other Aesir gods battled giants from Jotunheim. Thought systems were often well-organized and "logical," with everything categorized as fire, water, earth, and wind, catering to our overdeveloped pattern-recognition tendency even where no real connections exist. Personality traits and bodily fluids were added to elements - the four temperaments described individuals as sanguine (optimistic, social, associated with air), melancholic (analytical, quiet, earth), choleric (angry, irritable, fire), and phlegmatic (relaxed, peaceful, water). Sacred numbers included 1, 2, 3, 4, and the holiest - 10, their sum. When only 9 celestial planets were found instead of the expected 10, they invented the anti-moon, a parallel moon forever invisible. These examples show attempts to create intuitive-feeling systems. Using Kahneman's terminology, the "think fast" system immediately finds similarities and feels good about discovering patterns, unlike the "think slow" system that analyzes whether something is actually likely.

A recent phenomenon is fascination with "ancient wisdom" where Mayans, Sanskrit texts, indigenous peoples, or others supposedly hold superior answers and rituals (particularly appealing to disillusioned middle-aged executives and hippies). The idea that forgotten truths exist among indigenous peoples, often accessible through mind-altering drugs, is gaining traction, especially in Silicon Valley's new hippie-tech scene. This typically begins with recreational psychedelics, progresses to "psychonautical" consciousness exploration, and may culminate in Amazon journeys seeking "indigenous" tribes with secret wisdom. I have mixed feelings about this movement. It's positive that tired capitalists increasingly care about inner journeys, nature, and becoming forces for good. The spiritual guides are often friendly, inclusive, and beautiful, and some wisdom nuggets and treatments hold value. However, as a history student, I see mostly recycled 1960s hippie movement insights. There's often naive acceptance of unfounded magical claims, pseudoscience, and surrendering decision responsibility to shamans and "the universe," falling short of philosopher Immanuel Kant's call for us to become mature, thinking adults. I'm not writing to insult anyone's beliefs, but sharing my view that magical, escapist thinking can hinder healthy inner dialogue which, undisturbed by magical spirit animals and universal master plans, could make people much happier and more content.

Nature

One growing area is the almost religious attitude toward nature and "natural" things. This is undoubtedly fueled by obvious nature destruction through global warming, water scarcity, disasters, and polluted skies created over the last century. Opinions range from rational focus on sustainability and new industrial models avoiding planetary and human exploitation, to naive beliefs that everything natural is good and everything man-made is inferior. Some argue vaccines are inherently bad while shaman-provided roots are probably good. Organic tomatoes are automatically considered superior regardless of non-organic tomatoes' actual nutritional values, driving marketing departments to label everything from water to hotels as organic, natural, and straight from Mother Nature. I appreciate the increased sustainability focus and resulting respect for nature globally. I just hope we remember to think slowly when hearing terms like "natural" or "from sacred Mother Nature."

Cosmic determinism

"God does not play dice"

- Albert Einstein

An interesting idea supported by leading physicists and thinkers suggests that understanding the Big Bang and universe velocities might reveal everything following as natural, inevitable continuation of event chains starting with the Big Bang and ending around 20 billion years from now when the last star disappears. My understanding of universe physics is nearly nonexistent, so I'll avoid further exploration or explaining their reasoning.

The universe and its many spirits

Many friends are religious while others firmly believe in magic and various pseudosciences. What I personally struggle with is confusion between fatalism ("everything happens for a reason... so if I'm a suicide bomber I'm not responsible for innocent victims, God will welcome them as martyrs in heaven") and determinism ("everything happens for a reason - the child died because you blew up the bus and the family mourns forever"). Or another fatalism example: "We'll win the battle because Odin is with us" versus determinism "Vikings will defeat unarmed monastery monks because Vikings are well-trained and armed."

Those believing in spirit worlds, ghosts, magic, or religion sometimes argue that non-magical thinking is boring and "not awake." The idea that the magical world is real but not everyone can see or feel its energy or spirits masterfully counters other perspectives. And perhaps they're right. Believers are happier than non-believers, and almost all religions deliver higher overall happiness scores than atheism (unless they're active atheists, who might be equally happy since atheism can function as active belief).

An anecdote from a castle I co-own outside Stockholm illustrates this. The castle features the White Lady, one of Europe's best-documented ghosts. This creates significant interest, benefiting business, so I appreciate ghosts from that perspective. However, staff refused to enter the basement alone, requiring twice as many people because of the ghost, increasing expenses. The ghost, whether real or not, tangibly impacts the bottom line.

We emerge from thousands of years of traditions where belief in supernatural beings, gods, spirits, and magic formed the heart of all cultures and societies until the last 50 years, when more people began questioning the unscientific. I believe respectful attitudes toward others' beliefs and stories provide a good starting point, but it's probably wise to think maturely and slowly when magical wands are waved in ways potentially harming innocent people.

Conspiracy theories

A growing phenomenon is belief in conspiracies, increasingly common as media fragments and clickbait journalism spreads fake news and factoids while respect for media and journalism reaches historic lows. I've long been fascinated by conspiracy thinking and studied it closely. The (unfortunate) reason why many believe the craziest theories is that it helps powerless people who aren't comfortable with their life position and cosmic insignificance feel important. Some brains are structured to see patterns and systems where none clearly exist, making connections even when none exist. This group is more likely to believe conspiracy theories. Combine this with the internet's ability to connect like-minded people, and you have perfect conditions for conspiracy theories ranging from absurd to plausible but untrue explanations.

This was especially evident in 2021 when conspiracy theories surged from Congressional halls to Facebook and viral Instagram posts. Amid a global pandemic, conditions couldn't be more favorable for conspiracy theories. According to Cynthia Miller-Idriss, director of American University's Polarization and Extremism Research and Innovation Lab, people turn to conspiracy theories when feeling out of control, fearful, and anxious because these theories offer comfort through black-and-white answers. "When people feel out of control, they're drawn to things offering courses of action... It's easier to believe in evil conspiracy than an invisible airborne virus threatening their family."

According to Miller-Idriss, "unexplained deaths" - whether mass deaths like pandemics or famous individuals like Princess Diana - trigger conspiracy theories. "When something is terribly tragic, it's easier for people to believe it can't be true. They become more vulnerable to conspiracy theories because they may not psychologically process that it is true."

Every shocking global event, from Princess Diana's tragic death to September 11, 2001, generates similar conspiracy theories.

Unfortunately, politicians and business leaders have historically lied to citizens and customers about medical experiments, secret surveillance and torture programs, pollution, and weapons of mass destruction in Iraq. Sometimes critical thinking and skepticism transform into imaginative, outlandish willingness to believe information consistent with pre-existing political or ideological beliefs.

Some of America's favorite conspiracy theories:

- The Holocaust didn't exist or was exaggerated by Jews to get Israel.
- The CIA participated in JFK's assassination.
- The moon landing was faked.
- Princess Diana's death wasn't accidental.
- 9/11 was an American inside job.
- Mass shootings like Sandy Hook never happened and were media inventions.
- Top Democratic politicians run child sex rings.
- The Earth is flat.
- COVID-19 was invented (by Bill Gates) for population control.
- Area 51 in the American desert houses aliens (and state secrets).

Are we all living in a simulation?

A recent, surprisingly widespread belief suggests we're all living in a simulation.

Several arguments from Elon Musk and other thinkers support this idea:

- The simulation argument: Philosopher Nick Bostrom argues that at least one statement must be true: either all civilizations die before creating simulated reality, none are interested in doing so, or we're almost certainly living in a simulation. This argument assumes that if creating indistinguishable-from-reality simulation is possible, some advanced civilization would likely do it.
- Reality limits: Physicist and philosopher David Chalmers argues that our ability to imagine simulated reality suggests our current reality may not be "fundamental." Chalmers notes our limited understanding of physics laws and potentially unexplainable phenomena within our current framework.
- Simulation hypothesis: Elon Musk argues our likelihood of living in base reality is "one in a billion," and we're more likely in a simulation created by an advanced civilization. Musk cites rapid technological developments and increasingly sophisticated simulations as evidence we'll likely create fully immersive simulated reality eventually.
- The Mandela effect: Some simulation hypothesis proponents point to this phenomenon where large groups remember historical events or cultural phenomena differently from current documentation. They suggest this could indicate simulation errors or multiple simultaneous simulations.

- These arguments remain highly speculative and controversial, with many scientists and philosophers rejecting the simulation idea. However, the concept has gained traction among geeks and tech enthusiasts and continues generating significant discussion and debate.

Summary

- We love stories, and those we choose to believe shape our perceived reality.
- Some cultures, like the Burning Man movement or America's first settlers, more readily embrace magical or fantastic stories without scientific basis.
- What you believe provides an important starting point for using the Mindchange model because belief leads to a chosen truth system.
- People who believe in something, almost regardless of what, show higher happiness levels than non-believers (imagine how much better believers expect things to be after death).
- Those believing in fate, God, or the universe's predetermined plan risk not taking responsibility for their thoughts and actions, potentially making Mindchange thinking harder to apply, though no theoretical obstacle exists.

Thoughts to reflect on

Is there a cosmic plan from a higher power involving you, or are you solely responsible for your thoughts and actions? Try arguing against your actual belief - what arguments emerge? How does it feel?

Happiness, what is it?

HAPPINESS IS A complex emotion to define. Is it the intense pleasure of an orgasm, the contentment of looking back on a wonderful life, or the anticipation when dreaming about tomorrow? Is it the flow state when doing what you love most, or the satisfaction of knowing you're headed to heaven? There are countless attempts to define happiness, and I'll explore several of them below. The definition I use in this book is elegantly simple: "happiness is the happiness you want." With this working definition, I know you understand what I mean because it's your happiness (though I don't claim to fully understand your feeling or know if different people experience the same sensation). Using this approach, a Muslim imam can find happiness in communing with God in the mosque while a professional boxer finds it in the adrenaline rush of the fight.

One author who has profoundly influenced me is Swedish professor Micael Dahlen, who has written several insightful, entertaining, well-researched books on the subject. In one of his first works, Nextopia, he argues (with compelling evidence) that we're far more interested in what will happen in the future than what we already know. We love our iPhone most just before buying it and opening the box (which, incidentally, Apple engineered with slight resistance to create a ritualistic unboxing experience).

In the preface to Dahlen's A Little Book on Happiness, he explains he's studied how far happiness science has advanced and what we actually know. His conclusion? There's just enough solid science to write a "little" book on happiness—hence the title.

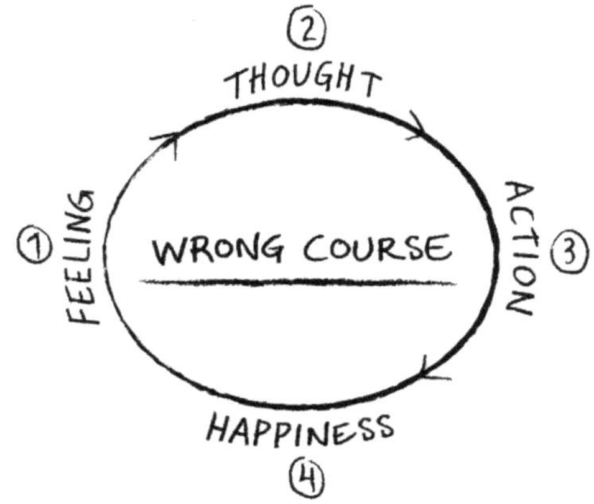

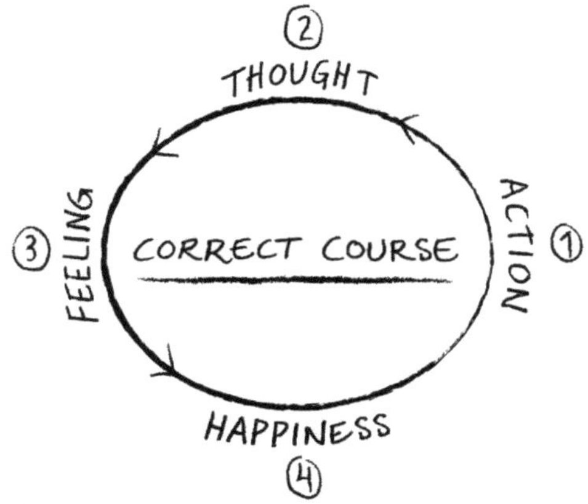

According to Dahlen and many happiness researchers, a significant portion of our "natural happiness" appears genetically determined—as much as 60 percent of our baseline happiness level may be hereditary. Research with identical twins and similar experiments shows DNA significantly impacts how easily we see things positively or negatively and how we process resulting emotions.

Happiness matters. Happy people enjoy numerous advantages beyond simply feeling good. According to Dahlen, they live longer, are healthier, make others happier, achieve greater success, and curiously, receive shorter prison sentences in court. In short, happy people live better lives.

Unfortunately, conflicting theories exist on how to maximize happiness, and many argue we should avoid directly pursuing happiness because the search itself is misguided. It's like forcing laughter and hoping it becomes genuine, rather than hearing something funny and laughing naturally. By this logic, pursuing happiness is equally futile because happiness results from experiencing the right things rather than being a destination itself.

Interestingly, when researchers ask test groups to measure their happiness level, the average actually drops just from the measurement itself.

The Dutch Jewish philosopher Baruch Spinoza argues that for most people, happiness stability and quality depend on what creates their happiness. What makes you happy determines what your happiness looks like and how happy you are. For example, if random events make you happy, you lack control over your happiness and remain tied to external factors. If you only feel happy when your sports team wins, they better keep winning. If cocaine makes you happy, your joy will likely be temporary, and your happiness pursuit will lead to many unhappy moments. If, instead, walking in nature makes you happy, you can do it whenever you want—and daily walks create more stable happiness. In Spinoza's case, this led him to avoid ordinary socializing, decline prestigious teaching opportunities, and even turn down wealth because he feared these would lead to the wrong kind of ambition and happiness pursuit. Instead, he lived simply, devoted to exploring thought and philosophy, and was by all accounts very happy. To me, this perfectly exemplifies how a

Mindchanger thinks and creates a personal happiness approach that works. Spinoza also admired ancient Stoic philosophers who believed people become unhappy by attaching happiness to easily lost things, making happiness equally perishable.

Spinoza believed worthwhile happiness comes from something permanent rather than fleeting, elusive goals. He created and determined what he found meaningful, defining happiness as a "blessing" where he developed a new "god" concept (though very differently from traditional divinity, incorporating geometry, theology, philosophy, and other elements in what's widely considered one of Western philosophy's most complex texts).

Many philosophers have wrestled with happiness, like John Locke who argues we must pursue happiness, but the solid, good kind rather than self-absorbed pleasure.

"The necessity of pursuing happiness is the foundation of freedom." But contrary to merely seeking pleasure, Locke's happiness pursuit must be "true and solid happiness, a happiness that makes us free from desires rather than yielding to them." So while your body might strongly crave chocolate, your mind knows that chocolate ultimately doesn't serve your "true and solid" happiness—your overall life quality and satisfaction.

Thus happiness isn't just pursuing pleasure, property, or self-interest (though it includes these). It's also freedom to make decisions leading to your best possible life, involving intellectual and moral endeavors.

These ideas shaped Western happiness views. Add an all-powerful God and you get the American Declaration of Independence: God created all men equal and gave them the right to life, liberty, and the pursuit of happiness.

Philosophy students might object to this formulation. They could argue: There's little solid evidence for "God." Obviously all people aren't equal—they have different sizes, minds, DNA, and countless other differences. Equality is a political aspiration, not an axiom. It's equally unclear whether "God" gave any creature the right to life, which seems more like a biological event. Whether all humans have freedom rights becomes complicated because "freedom" is complex and contestable. It's also curious that God supposedly gave Americans special status.

What about the final phrase, "the pursuit of happiness"?

For me, this is the most significant statement, actually making the other clauses redundant (though the declaration is an amazingly powerful spell catalyzing many positive changes). The beautiful truth is that pursuing happiness and living happily can happen regardless of living conditions, equality, whether God exists, or whether you're free—because this ultimately happens in your mind and can be developed through Mindchange thinking.

Positive psychology

A relatively recent science branch called positive psychology takes a different approach. Rather than helping mentally ill people feel normal again, it studies how the happiest, most positive, successful, and harmonious people function. What have we learned from positive psychology? First, we're all different, so different approaches work for different people, but some principles seem universally applicable.

One is having purpose. People with strong purpose generally report higher happiness. Additionally, experiencing flow while doing something correlates with greater satisfaction. Flow can mean getting lost in a video game, playing tennis, or simply enjoying conversation with friends where time flies. Another happiness component comes from "Hollywood moments"— "She said yes," "I won the World Championship," "I sold my company," or whatever creates peak experiences for you.

Having all three elements—purpose, flow, and peak experiences—seems optimal for most people. Having only peak experiences, paradoxically, can produce the opposite effect. Perhaps this explains why rock stars sometimes take their own lives. The hedonistic peaks or luxury lifestyles alone aren't sufficient—they need purpose and flow. The "Hollywood wives" from reality TV don't seem to be the world's happiest people either, despite their extraordinary experiences.

Looking at religion through this framework, almost all faiths provide purpose (you'll go to heaven or nirvana), flow-creating rituals (prayer, reading sacred texts, observing Ramadan), and peak experiences (God answering prayers, collective singing, or other transcendent moments). Throughout human history, religion has fulfilled these fundamental happiness needs.

In the past, culture also created strong norms teaching us how to think and behave. Today, people must figure this out individually, making it harder to find meaning, flow, and sufficient peak moments.

How happy are we (you) really and what makes us happier?

If I asked how happy you are on a scale of one to ten, you could probably identify a number.

Think about it. What if I told you your number is between five and eight? Am I right? When researchers have tested thousands of people, most score between five and eight. That's generally how happy people are—not the day before their wedding or a funeral, but their typical happiness level.

Ask these same people five years later, and they're still between five and eight, whether they won a million dollars, lost a leg, or experienced other major life changes. It appears we have a happiness set point or what researchers call a "hedonic baseline" where regardless of life events, we return to roughly the same long-term happiness level.

Isn't it disheartening that nothing we do seems to change our happiness level? But simultaneously, isn't it amazing? No matter what happens, our long-term happiness remains relatively stable. But there is one factor that can dramatically change your happiness level: how you talk to yourself.

Have you noticed time seems to accelerate as you age? Most people do, and one explanation is that we optimize our lives so completely that days become increasingly similar. We create life routines—picking up kids at the same time, training at the same gym, following the same schedule. As years pass, days become increasingly identical, creating fewer unique memories. Our perception becomes that time passes faster.

To test this theory, Professor Dahlen spent a year eating different lunch foods that no one (at least not him) had ever tried before. Unsurprisingly, he remembered his lunches better, creating more memories and mental timestamps, effectively extending his subjective experience of time. While this might seem counterintuitive, since time is a human construct based on perception and memories, having more memories than before makes it feel like more time has passed.

Our relationship with time affects happiness for many people. "I should be further along in my career." "I don't spend enough time with my children." "I spend too much at work." "I spend too little at work." Time is a complex issue and both a negative and positive catalyst, which we'll explore further in the time section.

The good news is you can expand your subjective time

experience by talking differently to yourself about time (or by watching less than the average 26 weekly hours of social media and Netflix that most people claiming "no time" actually consume). If you also define moments as happy, you'll remember them more easily as positive memories. Actively time-stamping and telling myself "this is a good memory or experience" has enriched my life far more than trying to optimize my schedule ever could. Going out and defining things as happy moments ("What an amazing moment, this is fantastic!") significantly increases what you remember. With this technique, you can have both a perceived happier life and an actual happier life with more positive memories—potentially twice as happy as without disciplined thinking. Imagine that! You don't need to win a World Cup or become a Hollywood star. You just need better disciplined thinking and self-talk, and you can potentially experience twice as many happy days, hours, months, and years as when letting thoughts flow undisciplined.

Another seemingly universal happiness enhancer is generosity, or what's called "giver's gain." When someone receives your gift with delight, you often feel happier than receiving one yourself. Similarly, gratitude appears universally beneficial. Feeling grateful makes positive self-talk easier and creates a more pleasant emotional state than feeling ungrateful. Studies show people who identify four things they're grateful for each night before bed experience increased fulfillment and happiness. This practice creates a positive mental timestamp making it easier to remember the day as good and worth appreciating. Something this simple demonstrates measurable effects on life satisfaction and gratitude.

Togetherness represents another crucial component. Historically, humans lived in groups of approximately 80 people in tribes. Without this natural structure, many feel lonely, and one theory suggests we have a primal desire for herd belonging and group context. Without this connection (common for many people today), people often include virtual connections with celebrities or politicians, making them part of a fictional tribe. The people you choose to care about become your tribe because we need community. With social media, this fictional tribe can far exceed the number of social contacts we're genetically equipped to handle, leading many to constant identity searching and stress as the tribe outgrows real human connections. However, setting aside the stress of oversized fictional tribes, relationships with friends and family fulfill an important positive catalyst function for most people, though these same relationships can generate conflict and unhappiness.

Meaning

Rather than pursuing happiness directly, many philosophical traditions emphasize searching for meaning. Meaning comes through fulfilling a higher purpose, not through simple enjoyment or an easy life.

A growing modern problem, closely linked to unhappiness, is purpose deficit and meaninglessness. Unfortunately, our increasingly affluent societies—making us richer, safer, healthier, more knowledgeable, and longer-lived—paradoxically make more people depressed. In prehistoric times, daily struggles for food, family, and security created natural, immediate purpose. Combined with strong religious and traditional structures, this provided long-term spiritual purpose and meaning that helped ancestors overcome life's hardships.

For me, the most incredible example is psychiatrist Viktor Frankl, former concentration camp prisoner who founded logotherapy. A brilliant Jewish psychiatrist who had studied

Freud, Hegel, and other masters, Frankl was finalizing his logotherapy approach when Nazis sent him to Auschwitz. For five years, Frankl endured some of history's deadliest, most inhumane camps. He witnessed the last humanity vestiges stripped from starving, dying prisoners while crematorium smoke rose. Forced into ruthless, predatory existence without dignity under constant betrayal threat, he lost many family members and friends. It's almost incomprehensible that anyone could continue living and seeking meaning after such trauma. In Man's Search for Meaning's first half, he describes Auschwitz life and suffering. In the second half, he analyzes as a psychiatrist who had a unique, morbid opportunity to examine human psychology's darkest corners, observing different responses to extreme situations—a nightmarish case study of human behavior no other psychiatrist had experienced firsthand. Miraculously, he survived through pure coincidences, like standing in the right line. He remained sane by creating meaning and purpose, thinking and acting meaningfully toward that purpose. His purposes included reuniting with remaining family, completing his work to share his unique perspective with all sufferers for eternity through publication, and helping fellow prisoners. His meaning quest maintained his sanity despite brutality and hopelessness. After release, it helped him overcome guilt, sadness, and trauma. Frankl didn't just survive—he used his experiences to create logotherapy, with growing treatment centers worldwide. Logotherapy assumes an individual's primary drive is finding life meaning. He believed happiness isn't necessarily the most desirable state—living meaningfully matters more and should be a fulfilled life's goal. This means regardless of how difficult your situation or suffering, you can always pursue meaning. Like in my case, when my father became paralyzed, I found meaning in supporting him, being a good son, and trying to make him happy instead of directly pursuing my own happiness.

Other famous thinkers like Freud believed we're driven by pleasure desire, and that desire and pleasure are our most important underlying drives. He believed our unconscious mind holds most psyche secrets, revealed through psychoanalysis. Most Freudian theories have been scientifically disproven, but several thinkers have found different underlying drives, like Nietzsche's and Adler's belief that "will to power" drives all humans.

Countless patients have benefited from logotherapy, finding purpose and meaning. I imagine how ridiculous a patient might feel discussing job loss pain or spider phobia with Frankl, who witnessed Holocaust horrors yet could confidently assure them he'd seen worse cases where people still found meaning and created fulfilling lives. Similarly, countless patients have been helped by psychoanalysis, hypnosis, years of psychiatric exploration, and other treatments. Interestingly, many methods like Freudian psychoanalysis lack scientific validation—no evidence exists and results can't be consistently repeated. Yet many people recover, presumably because they believed in the treatment and thus improved their self-talk, supporting the Mindchange model.

In my personal relationship with meaning and purpose, I believe meaning is a verb—something you do—and as you invest more time, heart, and effort, you become passionate and do more until it becomes meaningful. It's like starting a new job selling cars and suddenly having clear purpose, then climbing to sales manager with increasing meaning, purpose, and happiness until changing jobs to sell bikes with the same passion. Ultimate proof comes from soldiers voluntarily sacrificing lives for their cause, especially those without afterlife beliefs, like most Japanese kamikaze pilots racing toward certain death to hit enemy targets. Their Shinto faith emphasized this life rather than vague spiritual realms. They died willingly and purposefully, finding meaning because they—and their family's honor and devotion to emperor and country—mattered more than their lives. I've visited WWII kamikaze training centers in Japan and learned about their motives and pre-mission lives. One detail that stayed with me: they all wore helmets during their final, fatal flights.

A more inspiring purpose example comes from physicist Stephen Hawking's humble mission: "The complete understanding of the Universe." He writes:

"One, remember to look up at the stars and not down at your feet. Two, never give up work. Work gives you meaning and purpose and life is empty without it. Three, if you are lucky enough to find love, remember that it is there and don't throw it away."

In the Mindchange model, none of these approaches, including my personal perspective, is necessarily true for everyone. What matters is that schools of thought, chosen truths, and meaning pursuit can become catalysts for Mindchange thinking leading to increased happiness. Judge the theory's effectiveness by how it affects your life and happiness. For that to happen, you must believe in the model, just as belief in Jesus comforts true believers. One of Nazi Germany's worst criminals, Propaganda Minister Joseph Goebbels, was a fanatical Catholic until losing faith as a young adult, only to find it again as a fanatical Führer follower. In a diary entry he writes: "It doesn't matter what you believe in as long as you believe with all your heart."

This represents one of Mindchange thinking's most complex dimensions, and misinterpretation is easy. I'm not saying proven treatment models don't exist, or expressing opinions on God's existence or whether you should follow religion. What I am saying—what I experience daily—is that the highest purpose is talking to yourself in ways making you happy (happiness defined as the happiness you desire), and you can train this because the brain is plastic. How easily you can train depends on several factors like your negative and positive catalysts, chosen truths, and ability to embrace Mindchange thinking.

For me, the meaning search ended when I realized I could create meaning myself through internal dialogue. Armed with this realization, I returned to taekwondo and kickboxing after 20 years, training like a national team member. I consciously chose to become passionate about taekwondo after neglecting it since placing third in the 1991 World Championships before switching to karate and kickboxing competition. At 43, I became Swedish champion again and represented Sweden in two European Championships and one World Championship, facing many world-class fighters (who were twentysomething professionals living for the sport—and I admit my passion didn't help me defeat the world champion). Since then, I've won ten national championship taekwondo medals and became Swedish champion in All Style (stand-up mixed martial arts) in 2019 and 2021. My last final victory came against a hard-hitting 24-year-old MMA fighter.

Why share my martial arts experiences while discussing meaning? Few activities might seem as pointless as entering a small ring (actually square) to inflict and receive kicks and punches. But this example isn't about martial arts or even me. It demonstrates that when you act passionately about something, you become passionate. You don't naturally wake at night longing to comfort a crying baby. You become passionate about good parenting and being there for your child, transforming lack of sleep and difficulties into something beautiful and meaningful. The same applies to romantic relationships. Go home to your partner and try being maximally passionate for a week: breakfast in bed with champagne and chocolate-covered strawberries, enduring their terrible movie taste with a smile, writing love notes, showering them with gifts, listening attentively, and making them feel like the world's most loved person. What would likely happen (after convincing your partner you're not on ecstasy) is that they'll become more passionate and loving toward you, while you'll feel more loving and committed to expressing love. Again, I'm demonstrating that passion and meaning come from thinking and acting passionately and truly caring about something.

To further emphasize passion as a verb and its healing and goal-driving power, I'll share my latest martial arts adventure. One reason I returned to competitive training ten years ago was deteriorating hip arthritis from thousands of kicks. Doctors said I needed metal hip replacements and should forget future sports, especially martial arts. My only way to endure the pain (sometimes two hours nightly of tossing in agony) was creating a purpose driving me to stretch, kick, train, and ultimately fight. I did this for ten painful years, but my training kept me fully functional in daily life. During these years, Dr. Koen de Smet in Belgium perfected a new surgical model called the "sports hip" (or "Jean Claude Van Damme hip" after the action star who famously did splits between trucks after surgery). In 2023, my destroyed hip was replaced with a titanium upgrade. My recovery was arguably among the fastest in hip surgery history, attributed to physical preparation (training hard, fasting to minimize tissue and fat requiring cutting, planning for limited bathroom needs during early recovery, and other strategies) and loving friends who moved in and doctors treating me more like a Formula One car than a typical patient.

I underwent surgery simultaneously with my friend Michael, an experienced alpinist and climber. We supported each other, encouraged mutual healing, and coached each other through pain. My chef friend Derek came from the US to cook my favorite foods, and artist friends Anna and Nico from Poland moved in, making recovery feel more like a Burning Man camp than medical convalescence. But most importantly, I used Mindchange thinking to overcome negative thoughts, pain, and unpleasantness of having bone, muscle, and tissue surgically altered. Day one I was wheelchair-bound; by day six I discarded crutches. That weekend we celebrated with dancing. I felt intense gratitude toward my friends, awe for Dr. de Smet's skills, and optimism about soon sleeping through nights again. Two weeks later I returned to the boxing gym.

I set a goal to re-enter the kickboxing ring, and in May 2024 (seven months post-surgery) fought and won an international kickboxing competition in Tampere, Finland, defeating the 22-year-old Finnish champion in the final. This earned Swedish national team selection and a World Cup invitation in Istanbul, where for the first time I competed in my age category (40+) against masters and world champions. I won gold in one category and reached the Low Kick finals (allowing leg kicks). There I faced Mammadov Eduard, "The White Wolf of Azerbaijan," a 14-time professional world champion and one of history's most decorated fighters. I won the first round, but a broken rib, inadequate preparation, and his strength ultimately gave him the gold. Nevertheless, I accomplished my goal, transforming from wheelchair-bound to international martial arts competitor. The following month I won two European championship categories, competed in my first boxing matches against opponents in their twenties, and brought my daughter Evelyn to her first international competition where she won silver and qualified for the World Kickboxing Championships.

How was this possible? I genuinely don't know and wouldn't have believed it without experiencing it myself. I attribute both the healing and my ability to defeat top fighters in their twenties just seven months post-surgery to Mindchange thinking, which helped me focus energy, thoughts, and feelings toward my goals. Of course, it required training, enduring pain and hardship, and perhaps some talent, but the almost magical conclusion is that right thinking enables the seemingly impossible. And naturally, I'm preparing to face the White Wolf again, better prepared next time.

Summary

- Happiness can mean different things to different people, but there are universal "catalysts" facilitating happiness. These include finding purpose, experiencing flow, and enjoying peak "Hollywood moments." Generosity and doing for others creates happiness for most people.
- Socializing and prioritizing relationships is another universal happiness enhancer.
- What makes you happy (or what you choose to make you happy) determines how easily you find happiness. If you only feel happy landing on Mars, you'll experience less happiness than someone who finds joy in forest walks.
- Many thought schools and theories prioritize meaning over happiness, like creating purpose, though the meaning-creation process itself can be challenging and reduce momentary happiness.
- The Mindchange model suggests you create meaning through passionate action. Therefore, finding "objectively meaningful" pursuits matters less than feeling your activities are meaningful.
- How much is genetically predetermined versus created by living conditions remains debated, with Mindchange seeing default settings as starting points for disciplined thinking. Everyone can improve inner dialogue and increase

happiness regardless of circumstances.

- Everything in your life happens from now forward. There's no "going back in time," and you create memories in the present moment.
- Imagination is essential to being human, and allowing purposeful delusions or creating fictional mind games can improve self-talk, similar to how imaginary friends help lonely children or Jesus comforts devoted followers.

Reflect on the following:

What constitutes happiness for you personally, and how might you increase your happiness?

What gives your life meaning? What might happen if you began caring passionately about something currently unexciting to you?

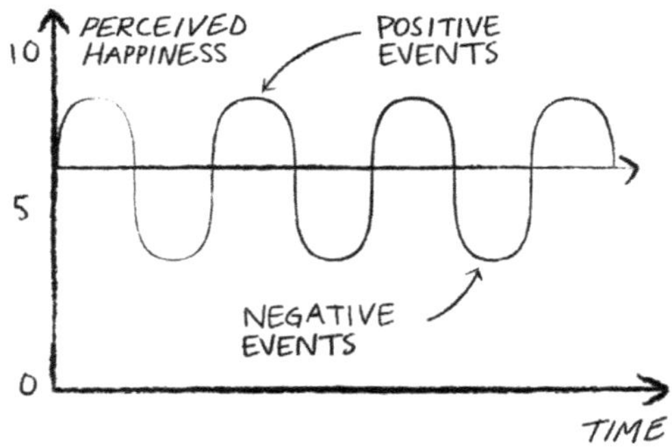

What mind games could help you achieve your goals? Maybe make a bet with yourself?

Think about a painful memory and try reframing it. Imagine it as a film where the soundtrack suddenly becomes beautiful, funny, or loving. Continue until you've found a completely different interpretation than your usual remembrance.

Prepared to be mindf*cked

A MINDF*CK IS a thought process where you experience your logic and experience occupying completely different realms, leading to new insights. It's also the working title of a TV series I'm developing to popularize the Mindchange model for the majority who'd rather watch Netflix than read this book.

Think about the last time you swam in a lake (or the ocean if you can't recall a lake). Visualize this memory. Go back in time and see it.

You see yourself going down into the water... NO. WRONG. You didn't see yourself that way. I bet you visualized yourself from an external camera angle as you entered the water. But that never actually happened. You never saw yourself from outside your body. This tells me several things about you: You're an artist who can paint an imaginary lake scene in a split second. You're also a designer who can instantly create swimwear. You possess all this creativity, yet that same creativity just fabricated your "memory." It wasn't something retrieved from a photographic archive in your brain. It's you telling a story right now based roughly on what happened, to the best of your ability. It's "based on a true story," but not the exact truth.

When you realize all your memories work this way—that you're creating films to remember experiences—you understand that you're the author of your life's book, the producer of this film. You can begin changing scenes you dislike and reframing memories through different perspectives.

Here's another mindf*ck: Think about your second-grade teacher. Was that person a good educator? Or not? Think about it... NO! Don't answer. You have no idea, do you? You were eight years old. What did you know about effective teaching? But now you've applied all your adult knowledge and wisdom, thinking fast as Professor Kahneman would say. You might even visualize the classroom with little you behind a desk, trying to remember that teacher, and it feels like that's what it actually looked like.

It's certainly not an accurate representation of what the child experienced, but rather an adult with all their accumulated experience constructing a memory in the present moment, based on what the child's frame of reference might have been in that long-ago classroom. This is central to the Mindchange model: understanding that how and when you talk to yourself creates your memories of the past right now, and similarly creates your future dreams. In both cases, you're the producer and therefore the creator of the memory, and you can use Mindchange thinking to become better at producing memories and dreams that make you happy.

When you grasp that most things exist in our interpretation of the world and inner dialogue, you begin to realize most of what surrounds us consists of invented truths. Money is made up. Being good or bad at your job is made up. Almost everything is made up. Even time itself. The concept of standardized time was invented in England because every village previously had its own local time, making it impossible to run trains on schedule. So in Greenwich, they established Greenwich Mean Time, beginning the era of common time.

You might assume time is the same for everyone. But stand outside in a freezing Minnesota winter waiting for a bus that never arrives, and time passes excruciatingly slowly. Spend that same period having a fantastic beach day with friends, and time flies by. Our perception of time varies dramatically across different moments, and with Mindchange methodology, you can learn to manage your time perception so you feel you have abundant time during enjoyable activities while less pleasant experiences seem to pass more quickly. We'll explore time more thoroughly in upcoming chapters.

It's never too late to have a good childhood

Everything in your future occurs from this moment forward. But everything in your past is also recreated from now onward as you reconstruct and newly create memories. If this is true (and fortunately it is), it's never too late to have a good childhood and never too early to be optimistic about the future.

I understand how incredibly provocative that first sentence might be for someone who experienced a terrible childhood. The idea of changing or reframing these traumas might seem impossible. My intention isn't to offend anyone, and I ask even the most skeptical reader to lower their guard and follow my reasoning, as this could initiate a healing journey where your perspective on a difficult childhood transforms into something more positive.

The realization that memories are reconstructions rather than perfect recordings—that they aren't identical to what actually happened—explains why even during lie detector tests, multiple witnesses often have dramatically different perceptions of the same event. This same phenomenon allows us to actually change our past by reinterpreting, attributing new meaning, removing shame, or even treating painful memories as "fake news" until they become less frightening.

Your memory forgets how it was but remembers the experience

Have you seen any of these movies? The Godfather, Star Wars, Sex and the City, Gladiator, Harry Potter... Most readers have seen at least one. If not, think of another film you've watched.

Now tell me how you felt that day when you saw the film. Were you sad? Had you been bitten by a mosquito? Frustrated about something at work? My guess is you have no idea. Most experiences store in our memory without any recollection of our mood or minor discomforts (unless you broke your leg the day before or experienced something equally dramatic). Let this sink in: The memories of what you do, even when deeply sad, will for the rest of your life be memories of a great film, or perhaps learning 100 new Spanish words on Duolingo, or gaining eternal knowledge of how to make world-class muffins or understanding Plato's philosophy.

When I realized this, it became a call to action whenever I faced a difficult or sad life passage. I understood that my future self would have all these great memories, and all I needed to do to secure these memories and experiences forever was to get out of bed and do things instead of canceling everything and feeling sorry for myself at home. This serves as a general antidote to negative thinking because when you do things, especially with others, the act of doing and thinking about things beyond what made you sad creates distance from the sadness and eventually helps overcome suffering.

This thinking model helped me counteract a bad breakup by training obsessively ("obsessive is what lazy people call focused people," according to an English Olympic coach), which later led to two world championship medals—bronze in taekwondo and gold in full-contact Okinawan karate. You don't need to go that far with a sport or obsession. You can channel your time and focus into other activities that prevent self-pity and disrupt repetitive negative thoughts by doing something—anything—where doing is the operative word.

A beautiful example comes from an American friend who grew up with abuse in foster care, lived alone in a car from a young age, and endured an incredibly difficult childhood. She eventually found strength to evolve and become successful in business and many other areas. But occasionally she's struck with overwhelming anxiety about her past experiences, almost becoming paralyzed. When this happens, she immediately stops whatever she's doing and orders Uber Eats for a homeless person in need. Simply by shifting focus from herself to someone else, she's discovered how to escape her anxiety spiral while simultaneously doing good.

Welcome to a great future

Worrying about the future ranks among our most anxiety-inducing activities. From "ugh, the dentist next week will hurt" to "AI will destroy humanity," some people tend toward negativity and pessimism about the future while others remain more positive, generally believing things will improve. Neither group proves more accurate at prediction, but the latter scores higher on happiness assessments and suffers less from negative stress.

Globally, we've never been better off in history. We live longer, cure more diseases, experience fewer wars, treat each other more kindly, and have become more equal, accepting, and concerned about human rights (though we remain far from perfect in many ways). On an individual level, both pessimists and optimists will occasionally be right because every life contains both difficult periods and unexpected positive developments. However, as you've learned, in Mindchange thinking, you author your own story and can decide how to view the future. Start by banishing negative thoughts like "I'll probably catch the flu this spring." With disciplined thinking, these negative predictions will gradually appear less frequently until they disappear entirely. With the same discipline, you can choose to focus on anticipated positive events and experiences, carving out a piece of the future and spending more time thinking about these possibilities.

Mindchange in theory

The Mindchange theory states that how you feel—and therefore your happiness—functions as a direct result of how you talk to yourself. Different people have different starting points for taking command of their inner story and becoming CEO of their thoughts and feelings. These starting points, or baseline happiness levels, are determined by factors ranging from DNA to worldview (philosophical/religious beliefs), chosen truths about important matters, past experiences both good and bad, your culture and historical period, and the stories you tell yourself. Additionally, everyone has negative and positive catalysts making it harder or easier to speak well to oneself. This creates your starting point, similar to an untrained person entering a gym for the first time. From here, disciplined Mindchange thinking begins, gradually creating better inner dialogue and higher happiness levels with the same certainty that muscles develop with consistent gym training.

Once you understand these components, it becomes an interesting exercise to objectively examine what belief systems and chosen truths you hold, and how these and their respective catalysts influence your thinking.

Imagine you live in a Muslim community, believe in Allah, have developed an alcohol addiction (which is haram and against Holy Scripture teachings), are overweight, and sleep poorly. Your family relationship has become toxic due to drinking, and you experience existential and religious anxiety, fearing God's wrath and the afterlife... Your Mindchange journey begins from this baseline where positive thought patterns are difficult to embrace and negative ones hard to avoid. If you managed to stop drinking, spend more time at the mosque, make peace with your wife, buy jogging shoes for both of you, and establish a morning walk routine that gradually becomes a jog on sunny days... your positive thinking catalysts would improve significantly.

Mindchange thinking doesn't prescribe how to think, but rather asks you to first analyze your current "factory settings" consisting of worldview, parents, chosen truths, culture, temporal norms, and past experiences.

Self-authorship

As you become increasingly skilled in disciplined thinking, you transition from being a victim of external events to determining how you interpret the world. You can decide how you react rather than suffering from others' words, and you can set your own ambition level without being enslaved by personal goals or others' expectations. You become solely responsible for your thinking and therefore your feelings, authoring your life story. In this self-actualized state, you're free to interpret the world in ways making you happy.

When many people hear this, they become skeptical, claiming you can't disregard society or others' opinions, and that constant happiness isn't a realistic goal. The truth is you can—just as J.K.

Rowling writes the next Harry Potter chapter without permission or concern for other authors' opinions, you can decide what to think and choose happiness even in scenarios others find challenging. Fortunately, we rarely face the extreme scenarios skeptics imagine, and it's even easier to manage self-talk in everyday situations. Miss your flight? You can choose not to get upset, take another flight, and recognize it's not the end of the world.

Mindchange is programming and reprogramming your inner dialogue

You now understand that the brain is plastic and your thoughts can be trained to create emotions. Here are some examples of transformational thinking:

From	**To**
I need healing.	I want to evolve.
I have to go back and find my traumas.	I want to realize my dreams.
I have a diagnosis that prevents me from ...	Everyone can evolve into anything because the brain is plastic and you are the author of your own life.

It's like learning computer programming. Based on what makes you happy, you can now program that state. But programming doesn't happen automatically—just knowing programming works doesn't create cool applications. Only methodically pressing keys that become code accomplishes that. Similarly, you improve at programming your thoughts and feelings with practice. If programming sounds too robotic, consider it a journey of beautiful discoveries where you learn more about your true self while taking ownership of your stories.

The first step is critically examining your worldview. Do your religious or philosophical beliefs obstruct your happiness? Can you challenge your view of predetermined personality traits or other chosen truths? What unhappiness sources in your life stem from cultural factors based on when and where you were born, and can you reframe them to reduce their negative impact? Then analyze your negative catalysts: Are you sleeping or exercising too little, eating poorly, spending time with energy-draining people? Do you neglect friends and family? Do you take unnecessary worry-inducing risks or pressure yourself negatively? As you learn more about negative catalysts in later chapters, you'll identify your own and learn to accept or change them to facilitate positive internal dialogue. Similarly, understand your positive catalysts making positive thinking and happiness easier, from friends and family to sources of pride, physical health, and mental strength. Reducing negative catalysts while increasing positive ones is the starting point and important firs steps on the Mindchange journey—and it works best when you're feeling relatively balanced rather than amid depression or trauma. The entire introspection process and understanding the building blocks underlying your mental states creates makes it easier to evolve and explore new perspectives on your way towards self-authorship and Mindchange thinking.

Below, you'll find practical methods for gaining perspective and improving thinking. This isn't definitive but offers a starting point for applying Mindchange thinking daily.

Leading with behavior

Emotions can be extremely difficult to control directly. The betrayal feeling when a close friend lets you down, the shame and anger when an unfair boss fires you, or deep sadness when your favorite team loses and gets relegated... For untrained minds, escaping such emotional states seems impossible—only time seems capable of stopping the loud, repetitive immersion in dominant emotions. These intense feelings often trigger repetitive thought loops seemingly impossible to interrupt, which may explode into destructive action or collapse into inaction.

With Mindchange thinking, you intervene earlier, building strong defenses that prevent the same negative emotional floods even during extreme events. When emotions do arise, you acknowledge them without fear, focusing instead on managing thoughts and behavior, which proves much easier than most people realize. You can behave like an athlete who exercises four times weekly regardless of negative feelings or anti-gym thoughts on the way there. This underlies cognitive therapy, one of modern mental health's most powerful treatments, and works even more effectively for everyday problems and challenges. Realizing you author your story and can decide your actions changes everything. When you consistently choose positive behavior, something beautiful happens: your thoughts eventually align with your actions, and eventually your feelings follow, transforming the experience positively as feelings, thoughts, and behavior harmonize.

Learning this approach to problems and challenges transformed my experience, making a positive inner dialogue much easier. Instead of letting feelings create thoughts that drive behavior, I apply "behavior that makes thoughts eventually support my actions, followed by aligned feelings." Rather than feeling gym anxiety, thinking others consider you weak, and therefore avoiding exercise, you decide on behavior—working out four times weekly. Let behavior guide you instead of initial negative feelings, and your thoughts become increasingly positive, creating budding pride that eventually allows you to think, feel, and act like an athlete.

Start with small changes, not an acute crisis

When beginning your Mindchange journey, start with small, trivial changes to train mental models. If you're consumed by jealousy over a potentially unfaithful spouse, that's probably not the easiest starting point, especially during relationship crisis. Instead, begin with your lifelong hatred of shoveling snow from your car each winter morning. Challenge yourself to become a happier snow shoveler, creating a mind game around your growth-oriented snow shoveling "career," and you might soon find yourself laughing while shoveling like never before. This success demonstrates the model works, enabling you to tackle more annoying chosen truths and situations until your overall frustration reaches all-time lows and you're ready for bigger happiness challenges.

As mentioned, starting a Mindchange journey during crisis isn't optimal, though accidents or terrible events may force this approach. When my father became paralyzed, he had no choice but accepting new life circumstances and finding happiness in remaining positive catalysts, revised worldview, and new positive chosen truths like becoming "the world's best patient" or coping because of exceptional mental strength. Adjusting during deep crisis resembles going to the gym with a broken arm—much harder than building strong muscles when healthy, which over time become strong enough to resist breaking.

Shift in perspective

Another powerful approach involves shifting perspective to others involved in problematic situations. This might mean considering the view and feelings (and possible underlying reasons) of a child you're scolding or the "idiot boss" who fired you. The exercise typically softens selfish focus on your feelings or thoughts. When my daughter and I visited Serengeti, she realized the leopard needed to feed its cubs, making the gazelle kill seem less unfair.

Another model is to create "the observer perspective" this can be fictional character and playful: what would your 82-year-old self want you to think or do now? What memories would you want at 82? Imagine wanting to confront someone who honked at you at a red light—what would 82-year-old you think about that? This perspective typically calms situations and has honestly prevented me from making stupid decisions. Simultaneously, it's encouraged braver actions than I might have taken following immediate feelings and thoughts. I frequently use another powerful perspective: "What would I teach my daughter in this situation?" Would I teach her to confront every rude driver? NO! I doubt you would either. With practice, these perspective shifts become familiar, and observer viewpoints guide you like conversations with wise friends. The growing gap between impulse reactions versus thoughtful responses makes you feel good about making right choices rather than regrettable ones.

Self-image – being in charge of your own feelings

Who would you like to be? How would you prefer to behave, think, and feel? Creating this aspirational self-version and emulating it powerfully changes behavior—like having an idol you emulate, except it's your ideal self. My self-image includes not being jealous because I value trusting partners. This isn't a realization but a choice—a starting point for continuous training. From ages 18-21, while engaged, I was intensely jealous. My memory suggests we both contributed to this dynamic as young people. The doubt, distrust, and searching for incriminating evidence felt terrible. Today I can't relate to those feelings because I've embraced different truths.

Now, my truth is never wanting jealousy toward someone I love and share life with. I would never investigate potential secrets or suspect disloyalty. I always believe and trust what she says, completely transforming my experience. It's been years since I felt jealousy's negativity; the opposite has become integral to my identity. This has cured the jealousy I felt as an insecure young adult. Perhaps I've sometimes had reason for jealousy, but regardless of external circumstances, I've banished that emotional response. However, this required dedicated practice.

I also don't get angry in traffic. I'm not particularly afraid of anything because I control how I view fear and manage internal dialogue. I've decided never to be lazy regarding my daughter Evelyn, which overrides any desire to sleep through her early training or reluctance to play in cold, wet snow after work. Anyone else might hear "sorry, can't do it," but for her I always override laziness with commitment. This reflects my father self-image stipulating I'm never lazy in parenting (though I don't always grant every request, just never refuse due to laziness or fatigue). Describing your ideal self mentally and articulating your behavior verbally helps self-coaching when needing future-self support. Avoiding grumpiness, prioritizing guests, or defending the vulnerable... you decide which hero you embody, and often that hero already exists within you, just a few actions and thoughts away. These examples show how projected self-image guides you toward right actions, thoughts, and feelings.

Mental models

Among happiness-increasing models, inversion is an established psychological method for finding happiness paths in situations. You imagine what would make you unhappy or frustrated at dinner or while traveling, then invert this to guide your steps toward happiness. If insufficient time with your loving partner would make you feel bad, build that into your experience. This technique transforms negative experiences into positive ones. MMA champion Nate Diaz focuses mental preparation not on positive scenarios and outcomes but negative ones, feeling prepared when even worst-case scenarios no longer frighten him.

Time travel

I remember my beloved Sensei Iryo often saying: "Ola-San, you should be here and now! Not here and there!" Today, we're frequently advised to remain present, which offers good advice in many situations. Experiencing the present with all senses has special beauty and, as mentioned earlier, represents the only time we're not producing mental films about the past or dreaming about the future. However, strategically leaving the present can be useful—letting your mind visit happy past moments or dreamy future events you anticipate. Like when Swedish travel agencies advertise "the journey starts here," this mental time travel, when done well, creates endorphins and happiness chemicals similar to thinking about loved ones (another happiness technique). With practice, you can travel backward or forward more quickly and clearly. As I write this, I'm heading to dental surgery in an Uber. I'm unconcerned because I know I'll mentally escape the dentist's chair to last week's Miami memories. I'll distance myself from pain and discomfort, remaining only vaguely aware during drilling procedures (perhaps feeling slight pride in my disciplined thinking).

Change the words you use

Words matter tremendously, as we've discussed. Our brains interpret words semantically, making our internal dialogue critically important, along with how we influence others verbally, which affects their interactions with us. I have a friend raised in abusive circumstances where family members suffered beatings and severe psychological stress. She maintained an active social life professionally and personally. At parties and dinners, especially after drinking, she often became the center of attention for empathetic listeners pitying her and expressing concern about her problems and ongoing difficulties. After developing our friendship, she asked me to mentor her and provide advice for moving from suffering toward a more harmonious and successful life. I suggested she stop discussing traumas and difficulties with strangers for at least a month, instead highlighting strengths and professional passions she wanted to explore. She accepted the challenge and experienced a transformative month with multiple job offers, new friends sharing her passions and ambitions and, most importantly, fewer negative thoughts and feelings because she lived more in a desirable future than a tragic past. This didn't erase childhood sorrows and scars, but it initiated a healing journey and transformed her life.

You see this phenomenon everywhere: the employee wanting to show the boss how hard they work and how stressful their job is, seeking recognition but instead convincing the boss they're overwhelmed and incapable of bigger challenges. Or the insecure middle-aged woman constantly mentioning wrinkles and cellulite to her partner, seeking reassurance about flaws her partner hadn't even noticed until she highlighted them. Words matter, and how you speak to others, even when sad or depressed, affects both your experience and others' responses. When a friend asks "How are you?" with a smile and you answer "Well [big sigh] not so good..." you begin cementing sadness. I'm not suggesting avoiding sharing sadness with friends—I strongly advocate getting perspective and support. However, I recommend avoiding routinely revisiting grief or trauma, instead pursuing positive conversations and experiences because they persist long after grief passes and facilitate moving forward and feeling better. Your memory, as we've seen, forgets your mood but remembers positive experiences, learning, and activities.

Change how you act and you will change how you feel

Words matter, but so do actions, because behavior changes how you think and feel. If you fear public speaking but do it anyway, continued practice reduces fear and improves performance. If you physically go to the gym and start lifting weights, you'll eventually feel proud and enjoy workouts more as emotions align with actions. Actions drive thinking which drives emotions. This also dramatically influences how others perceive you and interact with you. A surprising example was an old childhood friend who, despite many positive qualities, behaved like an arrogant jerk. In restaurants, he patronized staff when food arrived late or dissatisfied him. If someone bumped into him, he'd curse them out as "retarded assholes," and he always escalated conflicts.

Then something unexpected happened. My friend tried ecstasy, transforming his world. The drug released happiness hormones with effects including altered emotions, increased energy, empathy, and pleasure. He became loving and affectionate toward everyone. If someone bumped him, they received a hug. He couldn't stop complimenting hotel and club staff, and everyone became his best friend. No surprises so far—ecstasy and MDMA typically create these effects, as you may know from personal experience or research. The downside is depleted serotonin, causing mental crashes after the high that sometimes exceed the original happiness feelings, especially with frequent use. His outcome proved different. He had experienced a world where he treated everyone politely and considerately rather than contemptuous evaluation of others as servants or fools. In this new reality, people responded with kindness, laughter, and friendship, while conflicts became rare and easily de-escalated. He didn't take more ecstasy as far as I know—he didn't need it. He had changed his chosen truths and worldview, creating a more harmonious, happier life by his own description. He accomplished this transformation overnight rather than through years of therapy.

Another friend demonstrates acting like your aspirational self in a completely different scenario. As a UN Special Forces officer stationed with troops outside Timbuktu, Mali, intelligence sources warned that Al-Qaeda planned a full-scale attack to capture the city and declare a Sharia law caliphate. With only 50 elite soldiers as the area's sole military force, they received evacuation orders due to overwhelming odds. My friend searched his conscience and considered the men, women, and children facing enslavement in a nightmare scenario. He decided to stay, without requiring his troops to do the same—they could freely board the helicopter to safety. None did. Instead, they helped citizens build fortifications, positioned UN armored vehicles, and waited for approximately 4,000 jihadists to attack. When they arrived, the odds became brutally clear: jihadists outnumbered UN troops 100-to-1. Still, they held position, radioing the enemy that the city remained under their protection and UN sanctuary, warning they would fire upon any attempted entry. After a tense standoff, Al-Qaeda forces retreated and the city was saved.

I don't know what punishment my friend received for disobeying orders, but he earned the UN's highest bravery medal. Of course, he felt afraid and experienced negative thoughts, but through disciplined thinking, he acted according to his developed self-image where protecting the vulnerable outweighed personal safety. Later, when working with him at our innovation center Epicenter with thousands of members, his immense popularity prompted me to ask his secret. "I always smile at everyone when first seeing them each day. That's the only magic needed." Another example of actions creating positive thoughts in both himself and others in an upward spiral—and one easily adoptable by anyone.

Happy moments

A happy moment you just experienced might have been a wonderful future dream until you experienced the present moment. A happy moment that will become a happy future memory. The average person experiences approximately 26 happy years in their lifetime (we sleep extensively and feel alternately happy, sad, or occupied with other matters the rest of the time). Research shows that when you experience something and consciously define it as a happy moment, you feel happier in that moment and more likely remember it (because it stands out as a happy memory) and recall it positively. If you accumulate many happy moments to reflect upon, you'll experience your life as happier than someone who hasn't defined and cataloged memories in the mental album "My happy moments." This method can provide an additional 30 years of happiness according to research I've studied, and knowing you're reading about this creates a happy moment for me right now. I sincerely hope you and many other readers will adopt this approach and start creating happiness.

This is a happy moment. I will remember this and remember it as something happy. The beautiful thing is you can even travel backward in time creating happy moments, and you can forget things that once felt terrible, because you create every thought and therefore every feeling by speaking to yourself now and throughout your future life.

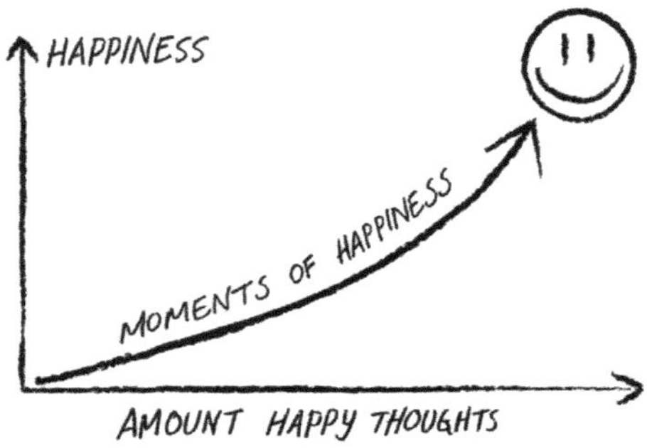

Summary

- We create more reality than most people realize, including memories which form now and in the future, resembling the film industry's "based on real events" rather than exact representations of what actually occurred.
- We can rethink and transform our view of terrible memories, redefining traumatic events or seeing separation, difficult childhood, or failure through new perspectives. As author of your life, interpretation matters most, not what actually happened.
- Creating an aspirational self-image and working toward embodying it powerfully drives development.
- Many mental models facilitate a better inner dialogue, including perspective shifting, revisiting fond memories, or dreaming about the future. Choose words carefully when addressing yourself and others.
- Thoughts and feelings follow behavior—it's easier to decide how to act than control feelings and thoughts directly.
- Actively identifying experiences and memories as happy moments helps you remember them positively and creates more happiness memories.

A dream

I have a dream where all children grow up learning to speak kindly to themselves. These children feel confident, curious, loved, and free from fear, anger, or sadness. They overflow with positive energy and curiosity. They know they can become anything they desire while remaining good and loved regardless. They experience this because loving, secure adults who have mastered their own inner dialogue raised them and are collectively creating the society they want for their children—a society where happiness becomes everyone's right. To feel content, proud, happy, purposeful, and fully alive with all the exciting possibilities the human brain offers for creating, experiencing, enjoying, loving, and doing all the beautiful things uniquely human. A society thriving with leaders who collaborate and manage increasingly complex challenges. Leaders who curiously accept building a "together society" instead of one divided into "us" versus "them." A society sharing both history and future vision where individuals collectively create better stories together.

The alarm clock rings and I awaken to today's reality. Now it's up to me to help make that dream real...

Barriers and Common Misconceptions

Self-deception or Mental Maturity?

WHEN FIRST LEARNING Mindchange thinking, most people stumble on this common misconception: "You can't just suppress your emotions! If you do, they'll explode later." This couldn't be further from the truth—unless you're a steam engine.

The reality is that dwelling on sad and frustrating thoughts creates chemical reactions in your brain that make you feel, you guessed it, sad. Likewise, positive thoughts, connections, memories, and dreams generate hormones that enhance happiness. Many people believe the plausible-sounding idea that trying to see things more positively means you're lying to yourself, or that there's an "objective reality" (which is always negative). This mindset keeps us locked in negative thought patterns, convincing us that changing our perspective is somehow dishonest or even dangerous.

I often hear this objection during my lectures: "What if you break your leg? You can't possibly think that's a positive thing, can you?" My answer is that we have the remarkable ability to think anything about anything. Each time we form a new thought, we build neural pathways that make thinking that same thought easier next time, effectively reprogramming our minds. My father's experience provides powerful evidence—after becoming paralyzed, which is far worse than breaking a leg, he created a happy life through Mindchange thinking. If that's not a compelling argument for this model, I don't know what is.

Another common objection: "I'm an emotional person, and I

could never go against my feelings." It's important to understand that as you develop expertise in Mindchange thinking, you don't become disconnected from your emotions—quite the opposite. Our emotional responses begin in infancy when we cry for milk, warmth, or touch. Growing into a wise adult means understanding our emotions while not being controlled by them, just as we don't burst into tears when we're cold or discover we're out of milk.

Instead of clinging to the belief that "I'm emotional and my emotions cannot be changed" (read: evolved), which keeps you on unnecessary emotional roller coasters or, worse, trapped in negative states, try asking "What if I could think and feel differently about this situation? How would this new perspective make me feel?" For example, when your elderly parents call with the same question for the fourth time, replace frustration with the thought that this is your opportunity to give back to the people who gave you life, comforted you through countless nights, taught you to walk and talk, and supported you throughout life. When this perspective becomes your chosen truth, you'll feel purpose and gratitude when that fifth call comes in. Mindchange can be this straightforward—and this powerful.

Labeling Yourself

One particularly destructive pattern is placing limiting labels on yourself. Negative self-labeling happens when you cement an image like "I'm not a public speaker" or "I'm terrible at math." This effectively blocks your ability to change how you think and feel about these areas. The words you use when talking to yourself stick, as we've seen in previous sections.

However, you can also successfully apply positive labels such as "I'm a quick learner" or the classic example of how far over half of all men agree with the statement: "I'm an above-average driver." These positive self-labels can be equally powerful and are explored further in the section on self-image—the version of yourself you aspire to become.

Labeling Others

We humans have a tendency to categorize people and slap labels on them. "He's flaky." "She's so uptight." Like self-labeling, this limits your openness to a person's potential and can often become a self-fulfilling prophecy. Consider the classroom experiments where teachers create an "upper" and "lower" group based solely on eye color. It doesn't take long before students start behaving in ways that confirm the worst stereotypes and develop genuine animosity toward each other.

Perhaps the most damaging thing that can happen to a child is being told they'll never amount to anything or that there's no point in dreaming. My father experienced this when he dropped out of school as a young misfit (this was before he became a Stockholm Mayor and member of the Swedish Supreme Labor Court). In contrast, English author Charles Handy writes about the opposite effect—when someone gives a child a "golden seed" by recognizing a unique talent or potential greatness in connection with an activity like playing piano or practicing karate. Handy's research shows that many successful people received such a golden seed in childhood. A golden seed can't come from a parent because parents are expected to praise their children. But a stranger or an adult the child admires can inspire big dreams and accelerate learning.

I remember the first time I sparred with a brutal-looking Arab man with long curly hair and a brown belt. His perfect sidekick sent me sliding across the floor, gasping for air. As a 14-year-old yellow belt with an inflated opinion of my skills, I had no chance of winning. But I got up and fought back as best I could. We began training together regularly and became friends despite our age difference and skill gap. I later learned that Rahoul was actually Indian, not Arab, and extremely knowledgeable about martial arts. After one training session, he looked me in the eye and said: "Ola, trust me: I know you will be a world champion one day." From that moment, I felt special and began comparing myself not to the kids in training but to international champions and my martial arts heroes.

Will Worry Make You Win?

Surprisingly, many high achievers I've met combine stellar performance with high levels of anxiety and worry. Their harsh, unforgiving inner voice constantly tells them they're not good enough, they'll probably fail, and their achievements aren't worth celebrating. When asked about it, they admit believing this mean inner voice is key to their success—that they somehow need it to push themselves.

This seems reasonable at first glance, but when you examine what science tells us about stress and performance, it's clearly untrue. These people succeed despite their inner critic, not because of it. If their inner voice had been kind, supportive, proud, and loving, they would have had more energy to focus on performance and achieved even better results.

I know this from personal experience. My inner voice was much more critical before I developed a loving, respectful internal dialogue. This supportive relationship with myself has been the source of energy and motivation behind all my achievements and the basis of my love for myself..

Becoming enthusiastic and taking a task seriously actually raises focus and performance. As stress increases, it eventually reaches a tipping point where excitement transforms into anxiety, and performance drops. When excited, you're working at peak physical and mental capacity. When fearful, you shift into fight-or-flight mode, and both muscles and mind increasingly lock up as stress rises.

It's crucial to understand that worrying accomplishes nothing. Worrying twenty times harder won't change your external circumstances. In fact, anxiety only makes things worse. Even when situations aren't ideal, we can still find another positive or constructive perspective, knowing we're doing our best and will continue to do so.

Default Setting

We all have instinctive ways of reacting to whatever happens—what I call our "default setting." As described earlier, this is partly based on your DNA, past experiences (both good and bad), the time and culture you happened to be born into, your worldview, and your chosen truths. There are also negative and positive catalysts in your life that make it easier or harder to take command of your inner voice and become the boss of your emotions and thoughts.

This default setting is analogous to a computer's factory configuration before you start adding personalized changes or reprogramming it. Similarly, your default setting is just the starting point for Mindchange thinking—where your journey begins.

Immunity to Change

If intelligence is knowing what to do, wisdom is actually doing it. So why is it so difficult to do what we know we really want to do? The sad statistics tell the story: people who start diets typically weigh 6% more a year later. The odds of successfully quitting smoking are stacked against you. And gym card holders far outnumber those who actually exercise.

I had the opportunity to study with Harvard Professor Robert Kegan, who has extensively researched this issue and developed both a theory and model for driving change, skillfully illustrated in his book with Harvard Professor Lisa Laskow Lahey called "Immunity To Change." Since this work significantly influenced the development of Mindchange thinking, I'll explore their findings in more detail.

Kegan and Lahey discovered that we have conflicting subconscious desires that function as an invisible immune system actively fighting against change, making us seemingly irrational. A person might initially engage fully with a change effort, but then inexplicably... do nothing. When this happens, the person may be suffering from "immunity to change." This goes beyond merely resisting or disliking change and can be much harder to understand and overcome.

This inner conflict can create a sense of being stuck or unable to make progress toward desired change, leading to frustration, disappointment, and self-blame. Kegan and Lahey's model for driving change involves identifying and managing these competing commitments to overcome immunity to change and move toward meaningful, lasting personal growth. By recognizing and understanding these conflicting desires, people can develop strategies to overcome them and make progress toward their goals. This process involves deep self-reflection, questioning assumptions, and exploring the root causes of these competing commitments.

Ultimately, immunity to change is a natural and common phenomenon, but by understanding it and taking steps to address it, individuals can overcome the invisible barriers preventing lasting change in their lives. In Mindchange thinking, immunity to change leads to holding on to negative truths, either consciously or subconsciously.

The Hidden Immune System

Kegan's Immunity to Change model starts by asking what single change would most improve your life. Next, it identifies and addresses competing subconscious commitments, aiming to overcome immunity to change and move toward meaningful, lasting personal development.

The model consists of four steps:

First, identify a set of personal commitments or improvement goals. When I took Kegan's course, my personal issue was wanting to play with and connect more deeply with my then 4-year-old daughter.

Second, identify behaviors that work against your objectives. When challenged to identify actions and thoughts that prevented me from playing with and connecting with my daughter, I was surprised by how many barriers I'd created. I joked about hating to play with Barbie dolls. I invited fun friends and nannies over to play with her instead of joining in myself. I didn't block out time in my calendar, so our play was constantly interrupted by phone calls. The list went on.

Third, answer this question: What uncomfortable feelings arise if you must change these behaviors? To my surprise, I discovered several stressful thoughts and feelings. "I'll be bored out of my mind," "I wouldn't feel authentic if I pretended to enjoy playing," "She'd have more fun with the nanny than with me."

Fourth, analyze which chosen truths underlie these uncomfortable thoughts. Again, I was surprised by my own insights. I had a clear chosen truth that she wouldn't enjoy playing with me, and this worried me subconsciously. I believed you have to be "real" with your daughter (but why should you be when playing make-believe with Barbie?), along with several previously unknown chosen truths that made it perfectly logical for me to avoid playing with her. When I challenged these chosen truths in step five and started testing games and activities, I discovered my chosen truths were complete nonsense—Evelyn and I had a blast together. The immunity to change disappeared when I chose different truths.

Kegan and Lahey found that changing our behaviors usually requires first adopting a more conscious and constructive set of beliefs. In Mindchange thinking, this means changing your internal narrative.

Let's examine this 4-step approach more closely. What would you most like to improve or change about yourself, and what's really holding you back?

1. Identify personal commitments or improvement goals.
2. Identify behaviors that counteract these objectives.
3. Identify competing commitments stemming from fears that emerge when you consider changing these behaviors.
4. Identify big assumptions—ideas you believe to be true without evidence until you question them.

Once you've identified your big assumptions, you can test them through small, safe actions that help overcome your immunity to change. By understanding and addressing these subconscious desires, you can develop strategies to overcome them and progress toward your goals.

Habits are normal. Change is difficult. We fall back into habits and semi-conscious decisions without disciplined thinking. Applied to Mindchange thinking, Kegan and Lahey's model helps identify chosen truths that conflict with what you really want, making them easier to overcome. It also demonstrates how structured approaches can powerfully support the thinking process and create positive change.

Thinking Backward or Forward

Believing things are fixed because of past events and that the only solution is to understand and solve problems by going backward represents backward thinking. Striving to think, feel, and act differently in the future regardless of genetic default settings and past experiences—believing everything happens from now forward—represents forward thinking.

Much of our explanatory style relies on backward thinking. If a child picks up an acorn and asks "what is this," we typically answer "it's an acorn, it fell from the tree" rather than "it's an acorn, it's going to become a magnificent tree."

This distinction has been profoundly important to me. People who spend most of their lives thinking backward, trying to make sense of real or imagined traumas, believing there's a secret in the past that can be unlocked through hypnosis or other means, generally find it harder to move forward than those who invest their energy in thinking forward, pursuing goals and dreams.

In relationships, backward thinking manifests as saying "you're always like this" or "you did this to me" instead of "I want us to be like this" or "wouldn't it be wonderful if we...". My entrepreneurial career has taught me to primarily think forward. This approach applies to many situations where I focus on pushing toward desired outcomes rather than dwelling on industry history, relationship backstory, or traditional methods.

As a friendly challenge, I invite you to see yourself without backward-looking labels or limiting assumptions. Instead, think forward—envision the future you want, who you want to be, and how you want to feel in that future. Another exercise: try avoiding backward-looking arguments in your next important professional situation or relationship discussion. You might discover you prefer this approach and begin applying it to your self-dialogue.

Passion is a Verb

Being passionate means engaging with powerful forces. Passionate love, passion for your work, hobby, or family makes us feel alive and connects us to our full emotional range. Passion closely links to purpose because a strong purpose often makes pursuing that purpose passionate. But passion can also become a vice, driving destructive or even illegal behavior.

A classic example of a crime of passion is a spouse who, discovering their partner in bed with another, kills the romantic intruder. Some countries have special laws providing lighter sentences for crimes committed in passionate states, as defendants cannot normally be convicted of first-degree murder unless the crime was premeditated, and a passionate lover cannot be expected to think clearly.

Setting aside negative passion (which Mindchange thinking can help control when you become the boss of your emotions), I want to focus on how to feel positive passion and act passionately.

I consciously found my way back to being a passionate athlete. As mentioned in earlier chapters, I decided to make a comeback in taekwondo, where I'd competed at world-class level in my twenties. It had been over 20 years since I stopped competing. This wasn't about a mid-life crisis but about my hip injury that doctors said needed surgery—after which I'd never practice martial arts again and would be partially disabled. My hip constantly hurt, especially at night when I often spent two hours trying to find a less painful position.

Rather than immediately having surgery, I wanted to try working around the pain through exercise, chiropractic treatment, and delaying surgery until doctors developed better surgical techniques or medications that could heal the joint.

During this exploration, I attended a taekwondo training session where students were preparing for the Swedish championships six weeks later. The training was enjoyable, and I still performed well, but clearly lacked certain skills and the stamina to truly challenge them—they were 20 years younger and elite athletes. I left the dojang (taekwondo gym) and returned to my office, feeling the pride that only a middle-aged man can feel after a workout, I stopped and reflected on why I'd lost my passion for taekwondo, karate, kickboxing, and kung fu. These activities had played such significant roles in my life but were sidelined as my businesses consumed most of my time.

In the office, a colleague and his guest stood at the coffee machine. "How's your wife?" my colleague asked. "We've been married for 20 years, so it's not the same," his guest replied. I felt struck by lightning. Of course—passion is a verb! I immediately asked the guest: "Excuse me, I overheard what you said and I'm curious, do you do the same things as before?" He replied: "Huh, what do you mean?" I continued: "You know, romantic getaways, breakfast in bed with love poems and flowers?" "No, not for a long time, you know, we've been together for ages," he answered evasively. He wasn't acting passionately, so he fell out of passion—just as I had with taekwondo.

Armed with this realization, I decided to become a passionate taekwondo athlete again. I signed up not just for the club but also for the Swedish championships in Gothenburg six weeks later. During those weeks, I trained once or twice daily, watched every match I could find, evaluated opponents, sparred with larger competitors, and when the big day arrived, I was as prepared as a 42-year-old could be in six weeks.

The tournament day was magical. I won my first match but felt rusty and uncomfortable. My second match was against the national team member in my weight class—on paper, I should have lost (thinking backward), but I didn't. During the match, I transitioned from confusion to flow and eventually won a clear victory. Three more matches followed, and I found myself in the Swedish Championship final.

My final opponent had dominated the other competitors in his bracket. He was Tajikistan's wonder kid, a junior world champion who had moved to Sweden and remained undefeated. My heart raced and I wondered what I was doing there. How could I possibly beat someone better than me in almost every way? Disciplined thinking helped me transform stress and doubt into determination and performance energy.

The match began, and we fought evenly, trading punches and trying to outmaneuver each other at high speed. He had a devastating back kick that threatened to crush my ribs when I got too close, and his timing was intimidating. I had stronger boxing skills from my kickboxing years but needed to get past that back kick to reach him. When the fight ended, I was thankful to have my ribs intact. I thought I might have won, but he prevailed in a split decision, making me the silver medalist in the Swedish championship at age 42.

I remember walking to the shower with my aching body and bruised face. I'd come so close to winning—just one judge away from being champion. I was frustrated. So close! I looked in the mirror and noticed my lower lip almost quivering like a crying child's. I started laughing uncontrollably. I realized: THIS IS WHAT PASSION FEELS LIKE. I, who simply wanted to extend my deteriorating hip's usefulness, had tricked myself into becoming passionate about taekwondo and won a silver medal against a world-class fighter.

Of course, I couldn't stop there, so I intensified my training, attending the "training camp for young talents and national team aspirants." A young guy watching me park my car said: "You have your own car, that's so cool!"—clear evidence I was probably the oldest person at camp. Through hard work, I earned a spot on the national team and represented Sweden in two European Championships and one World Championship. I faced world champions, European champions, and many of the world's best fighters in over 30 matches during the next eight years. I also won a silver medal in karate (why not try that too, since I was fit?) before winning two Swedish championship medals in All Styles, full-contact rules where champions from all martial arts compete in standing MMA rules.

Meanwhile, medical science advanced, and I underwent the procedure in Belgium that now allows me to move, dance, and fight without limitation. I then began my current kickboxing career, winning gold medals at the Finnish Open, World Cup, and becoming European champion in two categories, all during the first half of 2024.

Passion is a verb. The same applies to passionate love, passion for work, or hobbies. Try it yourself. If you're in a relationship, go home and create a passionate week filled with loving gestures and surprises, then see what happens. At work, set exciting goals for yourself or your team and approach them with passion, and with your hobby, raise the bar by not just showing up but taking it to the next level with passion as your fuel. See how it feels and where it takes you. Passion is a verb...

Summary

- As you learn disciplined thinking, you become the boss of your emotions, which then work even better for you.
- Common misconceptions about Mindchange thinking include the belief that positive thinking isn't "objective," or that it's wrong to override initial feelings. In reality, Mindchange lets you decide what's "objectively" better for you. You become the master of your emotions, directing your life with wisdom rather than impulses or immature emotional swings.
- A harsh inner voice or stress doesn't improve your chances of success—quite the opposite.
- Be careful about applying negative labels to yourself and others.
- Sometimes you resist change even when you genuinely want it. This "immunity to change" can be overcome by changing your chosen truths.
- Many people try to understand themselves by thinking backward. In my experience, you'll achieve more by thinking forward and creating the future you desire.
- Passion is a verb. If that's true, you can find meaning and joy by choosing to do something passionately. Try it and see if it works...

Negative and positive catalysts

THE MOST IMPORTANT insight of the Mindchange model is that how we feel depends on how we talk to ourselves. But as mentioned earlier, we're constantly bombarded with emotions and thoughts, making navigation difficult without proper guidance or training. In my quest to find the optimal path to happiness, I've read, discussed, and experienced countless situations where some people seem naturally disposed to happy thoughts while others are plagued by self-doubt, hatred, fear, and other emotions that make happiness seem unattainable.

What creates this difference? Beyond genetic predispositions, where some scientists claim over half our happiness capacity is coded in our DNA, it appears that generally happy people benefit from "positive catalysts" that facilitate positive thinking, while less happy individuals face "negative catalysts" that continuously feed them difficult-to-manage thoughts. This framework aligns with the "inversion model," which suggests that to understand happiness, we should identify what makes us unhappy and then reverse it. For example, if lack of sleep, stress, and guilt about neglecting your elderly father make you unhappy, try getting adequate sleep, finding support (or delegating responsibilities if possible), and visiting dad with flowers and his favorite cake. Sometimes happiness improvements really are that straightforward.

On a deeper and more permanent level, the same principle applies. Let's explore these catalysts, focusing on examples that seem universally true, though exceptions certainly exist and many powerful catalysts aren't mentioned here. Importantly, a catalyst isn't necessarily a fact. In Norse mythology, brave warriors believed they would dine with the all-father Odin in Valhalla's halls after dying heroically in battle. The chosen truth "I believe in Valhalla, therefore I do not fear death" objectively made believers extraordinarily brave, regardless of whether Valhalla actually exists. Of course, in other cases, the catalyst might be objectively true, as with "I'm sad because I'm allergic to sunlight," where a genuine medical condition creates negative experiences. Chosen truths and belief systems can act as powerful catalysts but are discussed separately since they involve relationships to thoughts or believed truths rather than life conditions or states.

Positive catalyst: a chosen truth, activity, or context that facilitates positive thinking and feeling.

Let me explore some catalysts that I believe universally benefit most people and have profoundly impacted my Mindchange journey – health with its components of exercise, sleep, nutrition, etc., along with love, family, friendship, and more. This isn't a comprehensive list or universally applicable to all situations, so feel free to identify additional catalysts using the same analytical framework.

Health and well-being

One of the most obvious positive catalysts is good health. A healthy body facilitates building a healthy mind. This works because exercise and sleep enhance cognitive abilities, and also because you spend less time in pain, worrying, or being prevented from doing what you want.

Achieving and maintaining health is conceptually simple but practically challenging. The main components are quality sleep, regular exercise, healthy eating and drinking habits, and meaningful human relationships. Though most people understand this, a majority struggle to maintain good habits and prioritize health. According to Harvard research, people who start diets typically weigh 106% more one year later—gaining rather than losing weight. As we've learned, immunity to change often means that despite knowing what's good for us, we lack the wisdom to consistently make the right choices.

A study highlighted in Jon Levy's TED talk reveals that health often correlates with our social circles. His provocative slide shows you're 40% more likely to be overweight if you socialize with overweight friends. Group norms regarding behaviors from tattoos to smoking exert powerful influences on individuals. People pursue health for various personal reasons—from looking attractive on the beach to living long enough to watch grandchildren grow up. What these motivations share is that nothing changes without action. To create positive health catalysts, I've established nearly automatic habits maintaining my health, including exercise hacks, sleep strategies, social contexts, and a personalized nutrition approach.

Exercise

Martial arts training has been a constant in my life, with competition serving as a life hack pushing me to train even when the weather is miserable, I'm exhausted, or my body aches from previous training (or occasional overindulgence). I'll detail my training approach and hacks in later chapters.

Sleep

Recent scientific discoveries about sleep have been as groundbreaking as they are impressive. In neuroscientist

Matthew Walker's fascinating book Why We Sleep, you'll learn about sleep's healing power (surpassing most pharmaceutical interventions), how deep sleep consolidates memory, and how REM sleep enhances creativity, potentially representing the evolutionary catalyst transforming us from apes to modern humans.

All living creatures need sleep, including primates. But why? Walker presents revolutionary discoveries about sleep's impact on every aspect of physical, mental, and emotional health, including creativity and longevity.

Unfortunately, most people in modern societies are chronically sleep-deprived without realizing it because we've normalized functioning at suboptimal levels.

REM and NREM sleep

Every night, your brain cycles between two sleep types: REM and NREM or deep sleep.

NREM (non-rapid eye movement) sleep features deep, slow brain waves that are 10 times slower than during wakefulness. During deep NREM sleep, you experience sensory blackout while your cortex (the brain's logical center) relaxes. Your entire brain focuses on distilling and transferring selected memories from short-term storage (frontal lobes) to long-term memory (rear brain regions).

REM (Rapid eye movement) sleep features accelerated brainwave activity resembling wakefulness. Your visual, motor, memory, and emotional centers activate, combining pockets of emotions, information, memories, and motivations into dream sequences. Your eyes move rapidly beneath closed lids during these dreams.

When awake, we constantly receive new sensory input from our environment. NREM sleep reinforces and stores this raw data and skills. REM sleep integrates these ingredients by connecting them with each other and previous experiences and knowledge, improving our mental model of how the world works, developing new insights, and solving problems innovatively. Essentially, sleep makes you smarter, healthier, enhances memory, improves muscle control and, unsurprisingly, enables better thinking and self-talk.

In Mindchange thinking, sleep represents a crucial positive catalyst, like exercise. With sufficient sleep, you dramatically improve your ability to talk well with yourself, and often tackling challenges after a good night's rest proves more productive than confronting them while tired. "I'll sleep on it" is genuinely sound advice supported by solid research.

Eating healthily

A nutritious diet forms the foundation for overall health—your body truly is your temple. Abundant literature exists on healthy eating habits, and generally consuming excessive sugar, additives, fat, and carbohydrates leads to poor nutrition and expanding waistlines. I won't delve into specific dietary advice since plenty already exists. However, I want to discuss food from a different angle because our relationship with food can trigger recurring anxiety, shame, and compulsive behavior, while simultaneously offering one of life's most reliable pleasures, available to most people throughout their lives. Developing a healthy relationship with food represents an important positive catalyst. This area typically features clear guidelines about beneficial and harmful choices, though resisting temptation often proves challenging, as Oscar Wilde noted: "I can resist everything except temptation."

As we'll explore in later chapters, you can apply both rule-based strategies (like avoiding sweets except on Saturdays) and simply behave according to your chosen truth rather than trying to eliminate thoughts about ice cream or cravings for chocolate muffins on weekdays. This approach becomes considerably easier when connected to your self-image and perhaps gamified with reward systems for following your plan rather than indulging.

Mindfulness

Meditation and mindfulness are well-established methods for calming racing thoughts and escaping modern life's constant demands. A MIT researcher friend who has extensively studied this field confirms clear evidence that meditation benefits numerous cognitive and physical functions. He explained that we continuously produce stories when reconstructing memories and planning future scenarios, consuming significant mental "processing power." It's only when fully present in the moment that we stop this production and think with greater clarity. Yet even "here and now" moments typically overflow with impressions, thoughts, sounds, and actions demanding attention, which is why meditation offers a truly unique and valuable mental state and deeper connection with our inner selves.

Mindfulness approaches range from basic deep breathing techniques for a few minutes of calmness to advanced meditations lasting hours. For our purposes, it's sufficient to note that moments of mental peace and meditative presence consistently facilitate better self-talk and improved thought and emotion management.

Having fun

Everyone enjoys fun, which makes it puzzling that so few people dedicate substantial time to it. Even more curious is how many default to the simplest entertainment options, like watching mindless TV series after series (especially when the remote control seems irretrievable). Children, in contrast, excel at having fun. They maximize enjoyment whenever possible, transforming tedious airport waits into magical adventures or converting tin soldiers into world conquerors.

For me, fun isn't a standalone activity but a feeling following engaging activities—like laughing because something is genuinely funny rather than forcing laughter hoping something becomes funny. In creative processes, playfulness lowers everyone's defenses and enables creative flow. Shared fun intensifies enjoyment and creates memories becoming future happiness triggers. Having fun promotes health, like laughing, dancing, loving, and experiencing flow. This is especially true when your fun doesn't involve excessive alcohol, drugs, or hedonistic pursuits that ultimately create negative catalysts or long-term health problems.

I believe our societies have forgotten much about genuine fun in our quest to appear serious, professional, and mature rather than childish. After prolonged immersion in corporate environments, only occasionally reminiscing about fun at reunions and never truly "letting loose," many experience meaninglessness and a melancholy "is this it?" sensation. What happened to our dreams and adventures?

Swedish band The Ark captured this perfectly in their hit "It Takes a Fool to Remain Sane":

Whatever happened to the funky race?
A generation lost in pace
Wasn't life supposed to be more than this?
In this kiss I'll change your bore for my bliss
Let go off my hand and it will
Slip on the sand if you don't
Give me the chance
To break down the walls of attitude
I ask nothing of you
Not even your gratitude
And if you think I'm corny
Then it will not make me sorry
It's your right to laugh at me
And in turn, that's my opportunity
To feel brave
'Cause it takes a fool to remain sane
Oh, it takes a fool to remain sane
Oh, it takes a fool to remain sane
Oh, in this world all covered up in shame
Every morning I would see her getting off the bus
The picture never drops, it's like a multicolored snapshot
Stuck in my brain, it kept me sane
For a couple of years, as it drenched my fears
Of becoming like the others
Who become unhappy mothers
And fathers of unhappy kids
And why is that?
'Cause they've forgotten how to play
Or maybe they're afraid to feel ashamed

To seem strange
To seem insane
To gain weight, to seem gay
I'll tell you this:
That it takes a fool to remain sane
Oh, it takes a fool to remain sane
Oh, it takes a fool to remain sane
Oh, in this world all covered up in shame
I'll take it to the stage!
So, take it to the stage in a multicolored jacket
Take it jackpot, crackpot, strutting like a peacock
Nail varnish Arkansas, shimmy-shammy feather boa
Crackpot haircut, dye your hair in glowing red and blue
Do, do, do what you wanna do
Don't think twice, do what you have to do
Do, do, do, do, let your heart decide
What you have to do, that's all there is to find
'Cause it takes a fool to remain sane
Oh, it takes a fool to remain sane
Oh, in this world all covered up in shame
Oh, it takes a fool to remain sane
Oh, it takes a fool to remain sane
Oh, it takes a fool to remain sane
Oh, in this world all covered up in shame
Oh, it takes a fool! (It takes a fool to remain sane)

In my chosen truths, fun plays an essential role. It's my top priority when traveling—I invest considerable time, money, and energy creating playful, fun, and exciting events, moments, and memories. These experiences give meaning to life's obligations and create a sense of destination. This explains why I attend Burning Man annually, spending 10 days with 80,000 participants in a co-created utopian experiment in Nevada's desert—an experience defying simple explanation. Wikipedia describes it as "a festival focused on community, art, self-expression, and independence held annually in the western United States," but that barely scratches the surface.

At Burning Man, "Ten Commandments" or principles govern the experience, not as dogma about how people should behave, but as a reflection of the Burner Community's ethos and culture as it has evolved organically since the event's inception over 30 years ago. Based on these principles, a microcosmos exists where no money, crime, unkindness, judgment, polarization, or negative energy exists, even if just for ten days. The cosmic glue holding this wildly diverse group together is the shared love and priority of having fun together.

Burning Man's principles are worth considering even for those who never plan to dance in the desert:

Radical Inclusion Anyone may participate in Burning Man. We welcome and respect the stranger. No prerequisites exist for participation in our community. This principle celebrates diversity and rejects the concept of "outsiders." In a world increasingly divided, the practice of welcoming everyone regardless of background, identity, or beliefs creates a unique space where unexpected connections flourish.

Gifting Burning Man is devoted to acts of unconditional gift-giving. The value of a gift is in the act itself, with no expectation of exchange for something of equal value. This principle fundamentally challenges the transactional nature of modern society, creating opportunities for genuine human connection beyond economic relationships. When you give without expectation of return, you create ripples of generosity that transform communities.

Decommodification To preserve the spirit of gifting, our community seeks to create social environments unmediated by commercial sponsorships, transactions, or advertising. We resist exploitation of our culture and substituting consumption for participatory experience. This principle stands in stark contrast to our advertisement-saturated world, creating a unique space where human value isn't determined by purchasing power or brand affiliations.

Radical Self-reliance Burning Man encourages individuals to discover, exercise, and rely on their inner resources. In a world of increasing convenience and dependency, this principle challenges participants to rediscover their capability and resilience. The harsh desert environment demands preparation and self-sufficiency, teaching invaluable lessons that extend far beyond the event itself.

Radical Self-expression Radical self-expression arises from the individual's unique gifts. No one other than the individual or collaborating group can determine its content. It's offered as a gift to others. In this spirit, the giver should respect the recipient's rights and liberties. Unlike much of mainstream society, which often rewards conformity, this principle celebrates authenticity and creative risk-taking, creating a vibrant tapestry of human expression.

Communal Effort Our community values creative cooperation and collaboration. We strive to produce, promote, and protect social networks, public spaces, art, and communication methods supporting such interaction. In an age of increasing isolation, this principle reinforces the human need for collective action and the magic that happens when diverse talents unite toward common goals.

Civic Responsibility We value civil society. Community members organizing events should assume responsibility for public welfare and communicate civic responsibilities to participants. They must also conduct events in accordance with local, state, and federal laws. Freedom at Burning Man exists within a framework of responsibility, demonstrating that liberty functions best when balanced with consideration for the greater good.

Leaving No Trace Our community respects the environment. We commit to leaving no physical trace of our activities wherever we gather. We clean up after ourselves and strive to leave places in better condition than we found them. This principle extends beyond environmental stewardship to a broader ethos of responsibility for our impacts on all spaces we inhabit, physical and otherwise.

Participation Our community is committed to a radically participatory ethic. We believe transformative change, whether individual or societal, occurs only through deeply personal participation. We achieve being through doing. Everyone is invited to work. Everyone is invited to play. We make the world real through actions that open the heart. This principle rejects passive consumerism in favor of active engagement, creating a community where everyone contributes to the collective experience.

Immediacy Immediate experience is, in many ways, the most important touchstone of value in our culture. We seek to overcome barriers between us and recognition of our inner selves, the reality of those around us, participation in society, and contact with a natural world exceeding human powers. No idea can substitute for this experience. In our increasingly mediated world, this principle calls us back to direct, unfiltered engagement with reality and each other, valuing the transformative power of presence.

These principles have inspired communities, businesses, and movements far beyond the desert, offering a blueprint for how humans might interact in more meaningful, authentic ways. They challenge mainstream assumptions about what's important and how society should function, providing a brief but powerful glimpse of alternative possibilities.

Love

Love unquestionably represents humanity's most beautiful emotion. It comes in many shapes and forms from parental love for a child, romantic passion, friendship love, affection for pets, patriotism, or religious devotion.

Without statistical evidence, I'd venture that love simultaneously constitutes the world's greatest happiness source and one of its primary unhappiness causes. Heartbreak, losing loved ones, or love's absence can create devastating wounds, depression, and despair.

Romantic love evolved from our hunter-gatherer ancestors' survival needs, where mothers required strong male protection during pregnancy. Human pregnancies last significantly longer than other animals', and our newborns remain helpless unlike many mammals that walk shortly after birth and soon learn self-feeding. From an evolutionary perspective, females needed bodyguards and providers while males wanted children but couldn't reproduce alone (and both desired pleasure). If sexuality and desire represent nature's reproduction mechanism, love ensures offspring safety, at least until mothers can independently care for them.

Romantic love theories are plentiful but with limited solid science. However, some interesting attempts to understand lovers' beating hearts and why we fall—and perhaps more importantly remain—in love exist. Controversial relationship expert Esther Perel, an American-Belgian psychoanalyst and couples therapist, argues that traits making us reliable parents and predictable partners diminish excitement over time. The nurturing dad changing diapers, handling dishes, and tending the garden can't compete with the sexy rockstar who whisks his partner away in a limousine during wild escapades. Simultaneously, that rockstar might not offer stability as a faithful husband and father. Perel's controversial solution involves infidelity and adventure rights—advice generating equal controversy and excitement in a world with increasing divorce rates and "living-dead" relationships.

An interesting study by behavioral scientists using both MRI brain scans and long-term interviews with couples concluded that for most, initial passion diminishes after approximately three years. The same neural pathways simply stop activating, and some couples remain together as friends, others for children or cultural expectations, while many secretly long for more passionate alternatives. Intriguingly, about five percent of couples maintained or increased their love intensity, with both brain scans and interviews confirming their love remained deep, genuine, and uncompromised. This reminds me of Greek mythology's romantic view of love. Greeks believed a hole grows in our soul when we're alone without love, and meeting someone filling that void creates love. They called this "human love." It fills emptiness, creating wholeness. But a higher form exists—divine love. Originally, we all had soul mates with unified souls. When gods witnessed this love, they became jealous, believing it too divine for ordinary people, and separated the loving souls who would forever yearn for reunion until reconnected. When you meet your soul mate again, no thought, evaluation, calculation, or planning is necessary—you're destined to reunite. My parents met when my mother was 13 and my father 16. They've remained soul mates ever since, creating the most beautiful relationship I've witnessed in fiction or reality. My own love journey began quite differently.

My first love experience came at 18, when I met a French-Swedish beauty and fell completely in love. We became engaged, moved in together, and believed in our eternal future. My chosen truth was that we were meant for each other like my parents. When we finally separated after three terrible years of fighting, breaking up, reconciling, hurting each other, and mutual unhappiness, I genuinely believed I would never find love again—that my only chance for experiencing parental-quality love had vanished forever. This triggered a year-long depression, while she engaged in self-harm and other destructive behaviors. I'm sharing this because love profoundly impacts overall happiness, and your chosen perspective on love dramatically influences how easily you find life and relationship happiness.

My next long relationship began six years later with someone so different from me that I couldn't initially imagine it becoming serious—which probably explains why I lowered my guard and allowed myself to feel again. Simultaneously, I realized my previous assumption that love happens once per lifetime was nonsense, and what I truly missed wasn't my miserable relationship but love itself. This relationship also ended after several years, but with positive memories and valuable lessons. A period followed where I moved from relationship to relationship, finding temporary love and friendship in romantic sprints and hedonistic adventures before finding deeper love with someone who was lover, friend, fiercely independent, and objectively promising as a potential mother for my children. We quickly integrated our work, social circles, and future plans. After several years, however, love transformed into partnership while our future dreams increasingly diverged. We realized shared values, friendship, and attraction weren't sufficient when dreams misaligned. We both hoped the other would adapt to our future vision, and as we recognized this wouldn't happen, we agreed to separate. We remain best friends and have both matured enormously since then. This relationship taught me that beyond sharing values, loving each other, constant companionship, and other qualities seemingly defining good couples, sustaining relationships becomes difficult with divergent dreams. If one partner dreams of eight children on a horse farm in rural America while the other pursues rock stardom in Los Angeles without children, separation or misery likely awaits. A more common dilemma involves partners dedicating 100% to careers with nothing remaining for relationships.

So how do you navigate romantic love amid these complexities? I'll address this shortly, but first, let me share additional personal lessons. After numerous trials and errors, a friend advised: "Maybe your odds of finding the right person don't improve by spreading yourself thin, meeting countless women and opening endless doors—maybe instead you should slow down, process your feelings, focus on one person, and fully commit to that single path."

Shortly afterward, while traveling in South America, I developed a beach exercise in Trancoso, Brazil that I optimistically named "Love Map." The concept is simple: take eight blank pages and a pencil. Create three columns on two pages (I'll explain the remaining six later). On the first page, column one details what your soul mate must possess regarding personality traits, abilities, characteristics, or life circumstances—from kindness to dog-loving to family values to vulnerability.

Be brutally honest rather than politically correct. If your soul mate needs particular physical attributes, humor, or financial stability, list them in column one. Column two includes important but non-essential characteristics. For example, I value dance partners but it's not deal-breaking. I prefer non-smokers but smoking isn't automatically disqualifying. Column three contains qualities you find charming and desirable but less crucial than columns one and two—perhaps "plays tennis" or "enjoys similar movies" (note that different people prioritize these traits differently; one person's tennis requirement might be another's casual preference).

On the second page, create similar columns for negative traits. Column one lists immediate disqualifiers—perhaps discovering racism or earthquake-level snoring. Only you determine your absolute dealbreakers, requiring complete honesty. Column two contains things you strongly dislike but can potentially tolerate. Column three lists minor annoyances you can easily live with, like "disliking his Dungeons & Dragons hobby" or "making you visit indigenous art museums."

Here comes the first mindf*ck: examine all six columns of desired and undesired traits, then ask whether your previous partners aligned with your Love Map. When I completed this exercise, it hit me like lightning that none of my dates or previous relationships matched what I claimed to want and need, and I'd accepted many things on my "never want" list. This realization was simultaneously comical and painful, highlighting my need for different thinking and behavior.

For the remaining six pages, I detailed how I needed to change myself and my behavior to attract someone fitting my Love Map, easily filling six pages with improvements that would have previously made me an impossible candidate. Importantly, I'm not suggesting changing yourself inauthentically to make someone love you or compromising core identity without integrity. Many people mistakenly believe they should be "loved as they are" without changing, rather than viewing love as an evolution catalyst.

Soon after completing my Love Map and implementing it as a guide, I met my daughter's mother, who became my wife and 12-year partner. At least ten of those years were wonderful, approaching the divine love Greeks described. Eventually, our future dreams and personal narratives diverged and polarized, making clear we couldn't mutually create future happiness as a couple. Strangely, from my perspective, what separated us involved our inner voices creating different stories making us incompatible rather than falling out of love (I remained deeply in love), but such is the power of internal storytelling.

The good news about Mindchange thinking is you can decide whether separation or staying together best serves your happiness, and you can "program" yourself to appreciate your choice regardless of initial sadness or failure feelings. The Love Map then requires updating based on current needs and desires, relationship lessons, and how you need to evolve to become an even better partner next time.

I've focused on sharing personal experiences to establish context for general romantic love conclusions. First and most important: how you choose to view love largely determines your relationships and relationship with love itself. My chosen truth is being a romantic who believes my soul mate exists somewhere, and I'll do anything for her and us when we meet. Another lesson: like negative and positive catalysts, finding love happiness becomes easier or harder depending on what love you allow into your life. Having a Love Map providing clarity about your needs, wants, preferences, and deal-breakers leads to better choices, transforming love into happiness fuel rather than toxic relationship heart-hostage situations.

What you need and give also changes over time for most people, and that's okay because you can develop your love with someone else (and according to Hemingway, you'll think back on the intervening time as "the good old days"). One ability you can develop with Mindchange thinking that most lovers struggle to implement is greater control over love itself. Having this power feels completely different from allowing passionate love to take the wheel and potentially drive off any cliff. I know this firsthand—as mentioned, I spent a year clinically depressed after my first breakup at 21, yet later danced away from my divorce with gratitude toward my ex and certainty that I'd finally be ready to meet my soul mate.

I've also chosen to believe that creating love together requires commitment and honesty, and relationships lacking these requirements aren't for me—I'm doing myself a favor by moving on.

Ancient Greeks developed words for different love types, from manic to unconditional. Consider these love definitions and how your love life appears when broadening the concept beyond romantic fixation. You might realize you have far more love than you recognized.

Agape - Unconditional love
Eros - Romantic love
Philia - Friendly love
Storge - Family love
Ludus - Playful love
Mania - Obsession
Pragma - Enduring love
Philautia - Self-love

Swingers vs stoning

As society grows increasingly complex, more people question traditional couple and family-raising models. A strong trend toward less monogamous relationships pervades the Western world, with "open relationships" involving multiple sexual or even romantic partners gaining traction. This partly reflects increasingly secularized societies where God no longer dictates morality or sexual partners (eternal damnation represents a steep price for one-night stands), but also acknowledges traditional models failing many couples. I knew a couple who prioritized maximizing their partner's lifetime happiness, then realized what each truly wanted for happiness extended beyond monogamy. At this crossroads, they chose including multiple partners and sexual adventures, believing selflessness represented love's highest form. Together, selflessly and lovingly, they created this relationship and genuinely lived happily ever after. From a Mindchange perspective, both individually and together, they created a narrative making open relationships not merely possible but desirable. Compared with traditional or extremely jealous relationships, their story differed dramatically. Where the liberal couple viewed ultimate freedom-giving as love's supreme act, the traditional couple would consider identical behavior as love's ultimate betrayal and proof of the guilty partner's unworthiness. I deliberately use "think" because both examples represent thoughts based on how they interpret the world. Each time these thoughts recur, they become easier to think and increasingly cemented in values and personality. For example, as a young man, I believed true self-fidelity meant following desires even when that included infidelity. I also believed no moral problem existed with pursuing someone already in a relationship. What you don't know can't hurt you, right? Wrong, according to my current perspective (though both moralities simply reflect how I talked to myself). Today, my self-image includes never wanting dishonesty, meaning I'd be dishonest with myself if I am dishonest to my partner. I also wouldn't cause grief or break relationships, so I'd respect others' relationships regardless of circumstances. My moral compass is centered on "who do I want to be?" and "what chosen truths create long-term happiness?" rather than external factors like society, God, philosophy, or others' expectations, which often drive such decisions. In extreme cases within certain cultures and religions, sexual infidelity or even rumors can trigger terrible consequences (especially for women) including daughters being stoned, honor-related violence, female ostracism, or at minimum social status loss. All these norms are constructed, based on chosen truths, and changeable. Therefore, examining your chosen truths and whether they move you toward or away from long-term happiness and harmony (based on your happiness definition) is crucial.

Let's talk about sex

Sex occupies more thoughts compared to how little most people discuss it. It's also a massive source of frustration and arousal. If any readers disagree, they might pause reading and contemplate steamy sex, then reflect on what feels most exciting. Historically, most cultures culminated marriage or bonding ceremonies with consummation before couples experienced sex together, with female virginity considered crucial. The young newlyweds would then exclusively have sex with each other (hopefully) until death parted them. However, numerous cultures maintained different norms. In many societies, slaves played often involuntary roles maintaining marriages, and rape and pillage have historically been common cultural features. In ancient Greece, homosexuality was normative, as was sex with individuals modern standards would consider children, and marriage to young teenagers. In Sparta, gender separation led to homosexuality, often involving sworn brothers-in-arms who were also lovers. Egyptian royalty married siblings and children to preserve the divine pharaonic bloodline. This means even something as fundamental as sexual preference can be radically influenced by society and represents more mental construct than natural, inevitable fact. The notion that you might be gay (or straight if you're gay), a rapist, incestuous, or pedophilic in different times provokes most people, myself included. But just like the classic example that anyone believing they wouldn't have been a Nazi in Hitler's Germany... most of us probably would have been.

However, certain biological facts remain undeniable—women can become pregnant without technological assistance. This reality and the physical, financial, social, and emotional responsibility for children motivated parents and brothers to protect daughters and prompted women to shield themselves. Another biological fact is our universal sexual drive, with individual variations in intensity. Some studies suggest men think about sex every seven seconds, while more recent research indicates men average 19 daily sexual thoughts and women 10. I'll admit falling somewhere between these figures.

In contemporary society, childbearing is no longer necessary, creating a dramatic sexual revolution liberating female sexuality while simultaneously generating global sexual pressure, frustration, and desire. According to the Washington Post, 28% of American men aged 18-30 haven't had sex within 12 months, with the corresponding female figure at 18%. Ten years ago, both figures approximated 18%, indicating fewer men having sex and many more desiring more (unsurprising when thinking about it every seven seconds without fulfillment for a year). This has spawned radical hate movements like Incel, a hateful, sexist online community for men who don't "get laid" and live without sex or romance. Several mass shootings have been perpetrated by vocal Incel members. Western male virginity rates are rising and testosterone levels dropping 1% annually. Dating apps like Tinder theoretically facilitate connections, but 79% of the most attractive women only "swipe right" on the top 20% of men, while most women receive attention on Tinder or during outings if desired. This sexual inequality creates a frustration time bomb. Another study asked couples about sexual frequency. Despite potential honesty issues, responses ranged from constant sex for new couples to biweekly for 4+ year relationships to rarely or never for a significant proportion. When asked how often they'd prefer sex if they could magically transport anyone to their bed, the average increased considerably—from at least daily for women to six times daily for men. While not Harvard or MIT research but rather a glossy magazine survey, it nonetheless demonstrates many, if not most, people don't experience their ideal sex lives. Some claim extraordinary numbers—Genghis Khan with 800 harem wives and Kiss bassist Gene Simmons allegedly having sex with over 10,000 women. I can't determine whether this indicates medical conditions or satisfaction with the latest conquest. As a sad counterpoint, sex-trafficked prostitutes can reach similar numbers while definitely unhappy about it. Most would probably agree that regarding sex, partner or encounter quantity isn't the appropriate measure—intimacy and love typically matter more. Nevertheless... sex means so much to us physically, mentally, status-wise, and in countless dimensions. I believe healthy, happy relationships with sexuality and inner narrative significantly facilitate happy thoughts and harmonious living. Since this isn't my sex-life autobiography, I'll avoid specific examples or personal stories, instead encouraging you to speak, think, and act in sexual realms creating short and long-term happiness based on your happiness definition. As friendly provocation for those never taking chances or embarking on sexual adventures opening new dimensions with partners or as singles, I've heard that many deathbed reminiscences cherish such memories immediately after crucial family moments and before professional achievements.

Love for your children

For many, love for children represents the highest imaginable love. I simultaneously agree and disagree. For me, love doesn't come in degrees, so I struggle with the statement itself. I don't compare my love for my older brother Jens in terms of "could I have a better brother." My love for him is absolute and in my chosen truth, real love is always absolute rather than relative to anything else. Similarly, I don't compare my love for my daughter Evelyn with other parents' love for their children, and I'm certain that with multiple children, ranking my love would be impossible. Somehow, comparing love devalues it, since comparison contradicts love's essence as an absolute feeling unrelated to those outside love's circle.

I personally experienced the same intense love and companionship with my ex-wife as with my daughter. The difference is that I knew it could change if we stopped actively loving each other. When we ceased being loving, our love ended. My daughter love, conversely, remains unconditional and unrelated to "how things go between us."

We love our children and they bring us happiness, yet several studies indicate parents actually report less happiness during active parenting—when awakened by screaming children night after night, washing endless diapers, retrieving discarded socks, and battling teenagers. Curiously, when asked about the overall experience, most claim significantly greater happiness and contentment since having children, contradicting their daily reports. To me, this again illustrates narrative power and experience interpretation (in retrospect) rather than objective experience.

Even regarding parental love, my chosen truth is that it constitutes an actual activity—the more you invest, the more love you feel. The doctor who delivered our daughter gave me the best advice: "Every moment with your child, from their screaming to vomiting on your favorite couch to demanding carrying until your back aches to staying home instead of dancing with friends, happens just once in both your lives. Seize each moment and fully enjoy it, because it never returns." Her words sustained me through baby years with interrupted sleep every 90 minutes for two years.

With Mindchange thinking, I create thoughts reinforcing my daughter love and reducing fears most parents experience, like health concerns or guilt about insufficient time (never my problem) or countless other parental worries. My chosen truths range from "I will never be lazy regarding Evelyn" to "I'm proud of being a great dad," and beliefs that both our futures will be amazing. My greatest challenge with fatherhood before I bacame a father was fearing freedom limitations. Then I realized that freedom for me as a dad means being with my daughter, much like freedom for a religious leader means being in sacred spaces rather than dancing on Ibiza tables. My other concern involved potential illness from birth and inability to give her a happy life. That thought vanished upon first seeing her—all that mattered was her breathing, and we would solve everything else together.

Friendship

Friendship is one of humanity's most beautiful aspects, but with so many different dimensions and types that it deserves its own section. Many consider their friends and relationships with them among their greatest treasures, on par with family. Some are even prepared to die for friends, as many brave soldiers have demonstrated in war and critical situations.

For me, it was mind-blowing to realize that who I loved and called friends had completely changed as I matured and chose my life path. The kids I loved and spent every day with at age 10 aren't part of my life now. The friends I spent every summer with at our vacation home are vague memories. My teammates from my first karate club I only see at occasional reunions, if at all. My high school friends and party companions from when I first experienced Stockholm's nightlife are now anonymous middle-aged people no longer in my life, along with business partners from numerous companies and countries where I've worked.

Yet at any of these points, I would have ranked these relationships among my most important, giving my life meaning and happiness. In some cases, I probably would have risked or even sacrificed my life for them. Now, living in several locations and thinking, doing, and being different from previous versions of myself, I have new friends—some from 30 years ago, others much more recent. The common denominator in my friendships is that we actively "do" friendship together. We create new memories, laugh, have adventures, and engage in exciting activities we both enjoy. Few old relationships endure simply because we were friends before. Even old friends need to actively practice friendship when they meet.

It's like when a friend decides to move far away for a job or relationship. You realize deep down you probably won't see each other much, but you're still happy for them, and as years pass, they fade into distant memories. If that same friend had died, or if you'd known you would only see them eight more times in your life, you'd be devastated. But why? The Mindchange perspective is that you would have told yourself a different story, creating a different internal narrative and thus different feelings.

This may sound harsh or suggest I don't love my friends or easily forget old ones. That's not the case. For me, it's a conscious decision to prioritize friends I actively engage with and exchange friendship with, but also a matter of practicality. I've lived an extremely social life and have between 5-10,000 people I'd call friends, depending on definition. If I had lunch with each, one at a time, it would take 30 years. My chosen perspective is that if someone doesn't prioritize me or we don't enhance each other's lives currently (which can certainly change over time as people and contexts evolve—one reason cancel culture is so misguided), then for a relationship to be valuable to me, energy must flow in both directions. If you're always the one calling your friend and suggesting activities, what would happen if you stopped? Painful as it seems, my conclusion is to leave or at least deprioritize such relationships to create space for people who love me.

So how can Mindchange thinking help navigate friendship's complex world? Again, you determine your own narrative. You can choose to enjoy friends, memories, future plans, and feeling part of a tribe that cares about you. As an exercise, thinking about friends with gratitude and remembering good times usually brings a smile and perhaps motivation to call and share your appreciation.

Loving Yourself

For me, self-love is beautiful and a foundation for loving others. It's also an important starting point for making choices and building a narrative from a place of beauty rather than suffering. The term "self-love" has been co-opted by many books and questionable theories about standing before mirrors giving yourself compliments or other Instagram-friendly quick fixes. What I mean by loving yourself is developing a deep, respectful, warm, kind, encouraging, and loyal voice in your head that makes you feel good rather than bad. We all have an inner voice, and self-love is the art of making that voice an ever-evolving, ever-improving companion through life.

If your inner voice were a person, would you want them as a friend? As a soul mate? As your child's best friend? As your child's soul mate? Too many people realize they wouldn't want to be around someone who judges, demeans, bullies, and negativity constantly. Yet they maintain this toxic relationship with themselves, creating many common problems. Having an inner voice telling you you're ugly and unlovable likely leads to behaviors making the prophecy self-fulfilling: jealousy, anger, possessiveness, or self-imposed isolation. Having an inner voice telling you you're terrible at work and an impostor who'll soon be exposed would make anyone underperform and doubt their potential.

So how do you create a loving relationship with yourself? As Mindchange theory suggests, each person's starting point or "default setting" differs based on genetics, culture, worldview, past experiences, and chosen truths. Whatever your starting point, I believe the journey begins with similar steps. Having experienced both a critical inner voice that was a poor friend in many areas when younger and my current supportive inner dialogue, I know the difference.

I began by making crucial promises to myself—foremost, never to be negative or rude to myself. This consciously chosen integrity was key and increasingly countered the voice's negativity. Initially, the voice would start implying negative things about me, but immediately the counter-thought "you can't talk to me like that" would arise, changing the narrative. Over time, I reclaimed the time previously spent worrying or feeling anxious and used this mental space to create positive dialogues and increasingly powerful mantras that built an ever-stronger foundation of self-love and positive energy.

Self-confidence and Self-esteem

Self-confidence and self-esteem are, for most people, two critical dimensions of living well. Let's discuss them separately since they're interconnected but distinct. Self-confidence is believing you can do something—confidence in your ability to ski, deliver a speech, or perform your job. Self-esteem relates to how you think about and value yourself. Many people, even at the pinnacle of their careers, lack confidence and fear being exposed as frauds. There's even a psychological phenomenon called impostor syndrome, involving anxiety and not experiencing success internally despite objectively high achievement. This condition often makes people feel like "frauds" and/or doubt their abilities.

Early in his career, boxer George Foreman won Olympic gold and became world heavyweight champion. He was mean, nasty, and cultivated a brutal image, developing tremendous physical confidence. His self-esteem, however, was non-existent, having grown up in violent, difficult circumstances. No matter how many titles he won or how much money he earned, he always felt worthless, angry, fearful, and depressed. After suffering a severe beating and knockout loss, he collapsed in the locker room, lost sensation in his legs, and was flooded with all the negative thoughts he'd known throughout life. He believed he was dying and welcomed death or anything to stop the thoughts.

But something unexpected happened—he experienced God speaking to him and showing him a new path. Foreman was saved and quit boxing to focus on helping others, eventually becoming a preacher and opening the Foreman Youth Center where troubled young people could develop the self-esteem he never had. After nearly 20 years giving away all his prize money, he ran out of funds and returned to boxing to support his charity. The media mocked the chubby, enormous 45-year-old stepping back into the ring. But they stopped laughing immediately when Foreman's superhuman punching power cut through the international heavyweight rankings and earned him a title shot. In the tenth round, he did the impossible, knocking out the reigning champion to become world heavyweight champion again. His victory earned him over $300 million—or rather, earned that amount for all the children and young people he helped with the money.

The later version of George Foreman possessed both confidence and self-esteem. He also had a strong sense of purpose based not on fear but on the desire to help those in need. The rest is boxing history. If self-confidence develops through an iterative process of creating an inner voice that encourages trying repeatedly, teaching that you never lose but only win or learn, and that failure isn't so devastating that you can't return and reach your goals, then self-esteem develops through that inner voice telling you that regardless of losing, going bankrupt, getting divorced, or whatever life brings, you are amazing, loved, special, and possess unlimited potential. Both confidence and self-esteem can vary across areas. I might have good self-confidence as a father but not when sailing. Self-esteem can also vary situationally, although strong self-esteem remains secure at your core regardless of circumstances.

Everyone can develop both self-confidence and self-esteem. Consider American Idol contestants who begin as insecure, shy kids in early episodes and transform into full-fledged arrogant pop stars by the end, sitting with feet on tables and wearing sunglasses indoors. They tried, they succeeded, they built confidence, they received attention and admiration, and their confidence grew. Trying many things, keeping what works, and improving over time without self-criticism when things fail is a good foundation for building confidence.

Regarding self-esteem, much of our initial "default settings" come from childhood. My dad had a tough upbringing, and his father was hard on him in many ways. But his father attended every hockey, football, bandy, or boxing match and most practices. If it was freezing at 10 below zero and only one spectator watched practice, Dad didn't need to look—he knew his father would be there, making him feel valued and loved. But self-esteem can be built at any age from any starting point. It directly results from the love and kindness your inner voice gives you. This development is easier with supportive people around you who appreciate you and in environments where you aren't judged or your worth questioned, but even in difficult situations, the basic path to self-esteem remains the same, beginning and ending with how you talk to yourself.

Professional Success

Being successful represents a dream and mark of greatness in most Western countries and many other cultures, though definitions of success vary culturally. I was once invited to speak at an event where artist Peter Gabriel and his friends had gathered a business angel investment club called I Gabriel (business angel Gabriel, get it?). After my talk, I led a discussion about success with the audience—all self-made millionaires or billionaires. "What is success?" I asked. After several rounds of discussion from different perspectives, the group concluded that the only success that matters to you is your own definition. Success might mean monetary achievement, where some people take shortcuts or even rob banks just for money. It can also mean the opposite—plastic surgeons foregoing lucrative Hollywood practices to help poor children in African villages rebuild their lives and futures.

Whatever type of success you pursue, having chosen truths and an inner dialogue creating harmony rather than an endless spiral of more, better, higher goals—whether results, salary, recognition, or book sales—is crucial. The drivers and definitions of success change throughout life for most people. Getting into business school was an important milestone for me. Getting out was another. Having freedom to manage my own time was vital at 25. At 30, I happily devoted all my time to my co-founded company in exchange for dreams of wealth, recognition, global domination, and making dreams reality.

The dotcom boom (and subsequent crash) offered a unique opportunity for young people like me to pilot untested digital rockets and accelerate full speed ahead. Boxman, where I was part of the founding team, sold CDs online and briefly became Europe's largest e-commerce player in our sector during the late '90s. Jeff Bezos, Amazon's founder, even came to Sweden, and we were invited to meet him (strangely, at the Vasa ship museum after closing—a museum commemorating a giant warship that sank on its maiden voyage in the 16th century, now our backdrop) where the then book-only online retailer described his vision of selling everything to everyone. I quietly whispered to my friend, "this guy has no idea how to grow a business," with all the wisdom of an arrogant 27-year-old. Walking away from that opportunity to learn more and potentially become part of Amazon's success story has since been called Sweden's most expensive mistake.

Later, I was invited to the World Economic Forum in Davos where, along with 100 other young men and women, I was named a Global Leader of Tomorrow. This incredibly prestigious appointment also provided access to the forum and ultimate halls of power, where a lunch conversation might be led by the Dalai Lama, followed by tea with Bill Gates and an interview with Paulo Coelho about his next book before a Lady Gaga performance or Bill Clinton interview. I had reached professional success heaven! But right there, meeting the world's most successful people, from politicians (I've met four US presidents) to artists, business leaders, and scientists, I began realizing that while they inspired me and seemed incredibly cool, I didn't want their lives.

I became increasingly convinced that success for me wasn't about focusing on one thing or sacrificing everything for it. Instead, it meant pursuing exciting untested ideas and grand visions with friends I loved, while maintaining freedom to be myself and do what I wanted. And hey, I had already made about 30 million euros before turning 30, so money wasn't an issue. At least not until the dotcom crash hit like a bomb, and everything I believed in—e-commerce, mobile phones, online communities, digital marketing, gaming—seemed to flush down the financial toilet of crashing stock markets and dried-up investor funds. I lost 99 percent of my perceived wealth in 6 months and faced financial commitments based on that wealth that I had no chance of honoring unless a miracle occurred.

Fortunately one did, when someone bought our Swedish

company Sportus.com because they wanted the SportUS.com web address, getting me back on my feet and allowing me to fulfill all commitments. When invited back to the World Economic Forum, I reached the same conclusion as before: I truly enjoy being myself and didn't want to base my life on chasing more and more success. These were crucial insights on my journey toward a better inner dialogue and thinking development. I don't worry about success or care as much about it or its rewards as many in my position do. I've co-founded 24 companies, achieved significant international success with several, and no longer need to chase applause or money. In a way, this represents a positive catalyst for me now, though in the past it functioned as both a stress factor and meaningful incentive. I've also long realized that others' definitions of success don't make me happy or fuel my passion (although dreaming, building, and succeeding always remains fun). I've married the idea that how I talk to myself matters more to my happiness than all the success in the world.

Summary

- We all have positive catalysts making it easier to see life's positive side and negative ones creating negative thoughts and feelings. By understanding your own catalysts, you can remove or rethink negative ones while strengthening positive ones. This creates the foundation for improved internal dialogue.
- Positive catalysts exist in many dimensions, with health being particularly important, including subcategories like sleep, exercise, diet, and relaxation. Love, friendship, meaningful work, and passionate hobbies represent other positive catalysts.

- Sex represents another important catalyst, an essential part of being human that can function as either negative or positive.
- In today's society, pursuing careers and professional success consumes most people's time and ranks high in many people's values. It can create stress and unhappiness or serve as a positive, meaningful catalyst. Understanding that you determine what success means and what matters in your life, rather than being hijacked by others' definitions and making yourself miserable pursuing success or money you don't truly want, is crucial.
- Self-confidence means trusting your competence and intelligence, with comfortable assurance you can accomplish what you set out to do. Self-confidence often increases with competence but also by not taking failure too seriously so you can try repeatedly until you succeed.
- Self-esteem means having a beautiful, loving inner voice making you feel you love yourself regardless of success or failure. Self-esteem typically develops during childhood, but Mindchange thinking means it's never too late to take command of that inner voice and build a loving relationship with yourself.

Negative Catalysts

THESE ARE EXAMPLES of common areas where negative catalysts make it harder to feel happy and content with life. So what are the corresponding areas that, for many, force them into loops of negativity and suffering? Below are examples I believe have general relevance, though as in the previous section, the list could be much longer. What matters for your own journey is identifying which areas of your life are negative catalysts and, once identified, deciding what to do to either change the area itself or your internal narrative about it.

Negative catalyst: a chosen truth, activity, or context that triggers negative thinking and makes it harder to think and feel positively.

Previous Experience

Terrible past experiences, lack of love during childhood, trauma, heartbreaking separations, deceased loved ones, humiliation, defeat, and suffering can each individually—and certainly in combination—torpedo even a born optimist's outlook and ability to maintain positive internal dialogue. But here too, Mindchange thinking works and can be transformative.

I want to emphasize again that I'm not offering a treatment method for severe trauma or PTSD, a miracle cure for depression, or a quick fix for self-harm. What I am offering is a method to gradually take command of your inner voice so it looks forward and supports your happiness rather than looking backward and hindering it.

There are two opposing schools of thought here. One believes in "thinking backward"—that our memories are fixed and remain part of our subconscious, controlling much of our present and future thinking, emotions, and reactions. The opposite view holds that nothing is "tattooed" on our mind or memory; instead, we create memories anew each time we think about them, influencing the memory itself. This "forward" thinking allows you not only to change memories and associated feelings but also to shift your perspective from primarily thinking about past events (thus recreating those memories) to thinking about what will be, your plans, and your future dreams.

As we've learned, our brain loves stories and excels at playing full HD movies in our minds that are visual, dramatic, and emotional. Having had an experience and thus a memory makes replaying that "film" easier because it's "based on a true story" (even though you're actually producing the memory now) compared to creating a vision of the future that excites, delights, or makes you feel good. Most people find it easier to identify reasons a vision can't be realized or the risks involved than to fully embrace and enter into that vision. That's why visionaries and leaders who can deliver them are so important.

How, then, do you handle past traumas and negative experiences that haunt your thinking and ability to speak well to yourself? The Mindchanger mindset is based on forward thinking, and simply realizing we all create our memories in the present and future is an important first step. Abandoning the notion that trauma is stuck in our cells, subconscious, or elsewhere is an important realization and first step toward owning your story. It's simple, but not easy. You can reframe the story and find ways to understand past experiences beyond the feeling itself.

I got divorced—initially a terrible failure based on my chosen truths of love, companionship, family, and loyalty. The thought of my daughter spending half her time without me and perhaps with some other "idiot" and his "idiotic" family was terrible. But reframing this experience with Mindchange thinking led me to embrace different chosen truths: it was good to break up because I wasn't getting the love I needed and wasn't living the life I wanted; I would be happier with my future soul mate. I also changed my original view of others entering Evelyn's life, believing another man and his family could add something beautiful, from different teachings to step-siblings and half-siblings. I transformed my initial concern about letting my daughter down through divorce into being the most present and engaged father possible, and our relationship is amazing in every dimension—better than when I divided my focus between wife and daughter. Having my daughter to myself now feels luxurious and right.

Some readers might argue, "Wait a minute, this isn't objective—you can't fool yourself..." They get stuck believing there are absolute truths about how you should think and feel about experiences like divorce, and that changing negative thoughts is somehow intellectually dishonest. It's not—it's the very foundation of Mindchange Theory and a power all people possess. This power can be trained and applied to any thought or situation because you, I, and everyone else has that inner voice interpreting what happens and has happened.

Anger and Grumpiness

"Anger is the punishment you give yourself because someone else has behaved badly."

Dalai Lama

Being angry and grumpy sometimes is part of everyone's life. However, it's one of the most dangerous negative catalysts driving us away from happiness, harmony with others, and success. In business, anger-based culture creates fear and devastates organizational effectiveness, as described in the section on fear. In relationships, grumpiness and anger often cause breakups or at least create conflict and "vibrate on a non-loving frequency." Understanding this makes it incomprehensible why so many people direct their strongest anger at those they claim to love most, are grumpiest with their children, or worse, most angry with themselves.

A common defense of (immature) angry behavior is that it's "real" and healthy to "let off steam" to avoid exploding. This may be true for steam engines, but it's untrue for human relationships or self-relationships. Instead, stepping back from anger or negative thoughts and viewing the situation from an observer's perspective often leads to better decisions and, naturally, a more pleasant day for everyone involved. Too many people also "demand" that spouses or friends love them despite their behavior rather than because of it—as if accepting anger and grumpiness rather than helping loved ones avoid negativity proves true love.

A useful mind hack might be thinking, "If I only get four opportunities a year to get truly angry, I'll waste one on this situation." Just by considering this, I regain my footing and can choose thoughts guided by wisdom rather than anger and instinct. Another less elegant hack is simply counting to ten.

Since caveman days, we've had radar scanning for dangerous animals or situations on the savannah, and our first seconds encountering new people or situations often focus on ensuring they're not threatening. If there's actual danger, our fight-or-flight reactions and reptilian brain often engage, guiding our thoughts and actions. If not, we're generally more open and curious about new people, situations, and experiences.

Another mind hack that frequently helps me in communication is the previously described situation-complication-solution model. The opposite approach—starting conversations with grumpiness and anger—triggers the other person's most defensive and perhaps worst side. Anger expresses itself not just through words or actions. Much of our communication, up to 70%, is non-verbal. A grumpy tone or angry face can trigger the same negative spiral as a verbal insult.

So what can we do when feelings of anger are boiling inside, receiving juicy suggestions from our brain to kill or at least scream at the idiot who angered us, betrayed us, or keeps throwing dirty underwear on the floor?

An important first step is checking your chosen truths. Most people I know seem to have adopted the motto, "I have a right to be grumpy... There's nothing wrong with being angry." I see it differently. When I see an angry child losing control and crying over minor things, I see someone I want to teach to think and feel better because it's obviously not a good state. I'm referring to immediate, inconsiderate, direct anger, like when a toy breaks, there's no milk for coffee, during traffic incidents, or when missing a flight—not thoughtful, values-based anger, such as feeling angry about Pol Pot's Cambodian genocide. But even with the latter, it's important to control your emotions rather than letting negative thoughts consume you, however righteous they seem.

As a martial artist, I've seen many fighters try building anger and hatred toward opponents before fights. This can serve as a positive catalyst for some fighters, but usually only at lower levels. The best fighters work with other mental states like gratitude, joy, curiosity, or euphoria as they enter the ring high on adrenaline and in the spotlight.

Being grumpy in public and toward people around you is like farting in public—not illegal but in poor taste and rarely bringing you closer to people. Words also matter greatly because, as you know, our brain responds powerfully to stories, and the words in those stories significantly impact us. Saying "What if we tried thinking this way, what do you think about..." instead of "You'll never get it..." when trying to change someone's mind makes an enormous difference. Facial expressions and body language are equally important. Up to 70% of all communication is non-verbal. If you're polite, smiling, and showing openness through body language, people react completely differently. Studies of job applicants who were actually trained actors show that confident body language and likable personality can matter more in receiving job offers than skills, and more than gender, race, or other potential discrimination factors. Yet many people have little control over their facial expressions, tone of voice, and how others interpret them. Or worse, they use body language to communicate anger and resentment without realizing the negative consequences.

In my journey toward avoiding grumpiness and anger, I work with powerful mantras (see the mantras section), the most important being my self-image: I don't want to be a grumpy person. Followed by: I don't want others (like a bad driver in traffic or someone flirting with my girlfriend) to control whether I'm happy or angry. I also know from experience that anger rarely leads to better or faster solutions to any problem.

To begin your journey away from being a grumpy, angry person whose mood is controlled by external circumstances, start with small things. Like not getting annoyed in traffic, at babies on airplanes, or when your elderly mother calls five times daily. I now feel clever when I smile after someone (clearly an idiot) honks at me in traffic. I hear a baby crying on a plane and think what a beautiful gift it is to be with a baby, then remember my daughter Evelyn as an infant (a champion screamer on airplanes) and enjoy watching the panicked parents oscillate between shame and resignation.

Time

Your relationship with time can be a major source of negative or positive thoughts. In Mindchange thinking, managing this relationship is a powerful tool. Are you living in old memories from the past or afraid of aging? Do you think you spend too little time with your children or at work, causing stress? Most readers can relate to time-related issues and time perception.

One of my favorite authors, Bodil Jönsson, an 80+-year-old Swedish physicist and writer, offers a wonderful exploration of time perspectives, concluding that time exists much more in our perception than as absolute fact. The perception of time matters more than the actual minutes and hours passing. If you're in the boxing ring with Mike Tyson, a second feels eternal and a minute lasts forever. If you're lost in the flow state playing your favorite video game, a minute passes like a millisecond.

We each have roughly 30,000 days to live, and how we view this time can be either a negative or positive catalyst. The Greeks distinguished between Kronos and Kairos. Kronos represents clock time, measurable in minutes and hours that tick inexorably forward. Kairos is the time when conditions are right for decisive action: the opportune, decisive moment. Kairos involves interpretation of time rather than clock movement.

British philosopher Bertrand Russell identifies our relationship with time as one of the most common reasons people feel unhappy and dissatisfied. Not spending enough time with children, never having time to read, not being where you want to be in your career despite years of work. Stress from running late. The feeling that time passes faster and faster. You probably recognize many of these thoughts and intuitively feel we cannot change time because its constant tick-tock lies beyond our control.

Let me offer a different perspective, starting with the realization that time is actually a human invention. Time is highly subjective. In his book "Numbermania," Micael Dahlen points to a study showing that on average we "feel" 8 years younger than our actual age. You're 49 but feel 41. Interestingly, this changes at even-numbered birthdays, so a 50-year-old feels only 4 years younger until turning 51, when they happily feel 8 years younger again.

Remember how much time we spend on Netflix, Facebook, TV, or other entertainment? 20-30 hours weekly... Many who claim they don't have time to exercise four hours weekly or learn a new language two hours weekly spend far more time on passive entertainment. From this reasoning, we can conclude that time and our relationship to it is a mental construct largely determined by how we think about time.

So how can you use Mindchange thinking to prevent time from becoming a negative catalyst? I'll answer by sharing my own mental models for common time-related thoughts, starting with stress. There's a popular narrative that our era is the most stressful, and women's magazines particularly portray today's woman, who must work, pick up kids, look attractive, and be a good partner, as a victim of terrible daily stress. This isn't objectively true compared to Medieval stress—5% child mortality rates (when women typically had 8+ children), Viking raids, extreme inequality, witch-burning risks, and fear of eternal hellfire. But it can feel true if you believe and internalize that narrative. This example illustrates how the inner dialogue creates stress, but as the next examples show, it can also do the opposite in stressful situations.

I understand stress well, having produced hundreds of events, spoken at many more, and taken over 1,000 professional flights—flights that tend to depart without me if I'm late. To maintain sanity, I use powerful mental "spells." I tell myself, "Only I can stress myself," and through this thought regain control as my heart rate normalizes. The next spell, "What's the worst that can happen?" makes missing a plane or being late for a speech less catastrophic and, in cosmic context, not worth any negative thoughts.

Bodil Jönsson presents an interesting thought experiment in her excellent book "Gott om tid" (Plenty of Time), imagining our wallet has four pockets containing work, education, socializing with friends and family, and internal time for thinking and feeling.

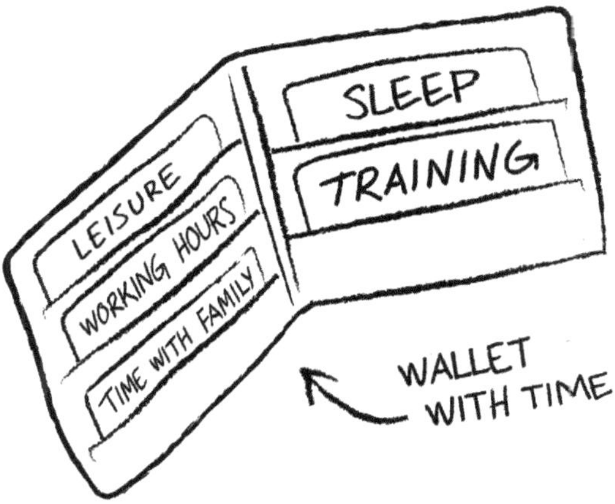

Since you can't simply exchange a unit of friend time for a unit of learning, she suggests time rather than money as the currency. How would you allocate your asset—your 112 waking weekly hours—between these activities? What could you do to free up more time for what truly matters to you? She concludes we all have abundant time if we learn to use it for what we want and develop the right relationship with both past time and the plentiful time we all possess.

A.G.E.

I used to lift weights with my Slovenian friend, who's exceptionally strong and stubborn. One day he failed to lift his usual weight and cursed loudly. I said, "Come on, you can do it," but he looked me in the eye seriously and said: "I can't do it anymore—I have a terminal illness." Shocked, I asked what it was, and he said he suffered from A.G.E. "What the hell is that?!" I shouted. He smiled, slapped my shoulder, and said A.G.E.— "age"—we won't get out of life alive.

Regarding age and aging, many if not most people struggle with passing years, at least during certain life phases. I remember spending most of my youth just wanting to get older as quickly as possible, even lying about my age. Now my mantra is "Youth is playfulness; you don't stop dancing because you get old, you get old because you stop dancing." Since I can choose to remain playful and keep dancing, age isn't so frightening. Another comforting thought: "Every year has been better—I look forward to the next."

I once met a fascinating, beautiful woman in her 40s who shared stories of her life filled with exciting missions, travels, and experiences. Halfway through our meeting, I began suspecting her stories weren't true—they would have required more time than her professional years, and some events occurred before her time. To expose the obvious lie, I started by asking her age. She turned out to be 68, and her stories were true. I've never seen anyone look so much younger in body and spirit (though Demi Moore at 55 came close when I was a +1 at dinner with her). Curiosity took over, and I asked, "What's your secret?" She smiled and said, "I think, 'What would I do if I didn't know my age?' and with that as my guide, I flirt with the young tennis coach, sign up for Mount Everest expeditions, choose friends, and buy clothes I like." A perfect example of Mindchange thinking.

Bodil Jönsson's time perspectives challenge the notion that aging makes life progressively less rich, colorful, and exciting. She argues the opposite because, having lived longer, we accumulate more experiences, can reflect from a larger smorgasbord of thoughts and feelings, and become better at determining the quality of our experiences. Much like a botanist who sees every aspect of different grass types and knows all the flowers and insects, while teenagers just see grass. She also firmly states that we do NOT have too little time in our lives—on the contrary, we all have an abundance. Trading that time for TikTok, work, commuting, or reading is all about choices we can make better as we improve at managing our time abundance.

TTT—time takes time. Reflecting on and learning to manage different types of time—time to unwind and relax, time to focus without interruption, traveling back to happy memories or dreaming of future times—all require time and conscious effort, just as TTT thinking takes time in Mindchange thinking. An athlete needs to practice; so does a thinker who wants to improve thinking quality.

Fear

"The opposite of love is not hate, it's fear!"

Yoko Ono

A terrifying negative catalyst is fear itself. Fear is part of our genetic makeup, a mechanism protecting us from danger and keeping us on the safe side of life's hazards. However, in today's society, fear has become more like a disease creating personal, interpersonal, international, and many other conflicts.

I believe the amount of worry or fear we experience is partly genetic but largely transmitted from parent to child. We love our young children so much that we can't bear seeing them fall when taking first steps, so we shout "pooor baaaby" with facial expressions suggesting serious danger.

To distinguish between fear as a healthy alarm against danger and fear as an emotion without proportional threat, I'll quote Dr. Mouna Esmaeilzadeh, who differentiates between fear of real danger and fear of perceived danger. Real dangers include undergoing heart surgery, fighting in war, swimming with great white sharks, or any situation with genuine risk. Perceived danger, conversely, includes any situation that feels scary but isn't, such as going into a dark basement, riding roller coasters, holding harmless spiders, or watching horror movies.

Our brains initially respond similarly to both, but with Mindchange thinking, they eventually separate into clear categories, where things that only feel dangerous but aren't become easy to overcome and soon disappear from the fear alarm system. Fear of genuinely dangerous things serves as a warning bell for our conscious mind, which can then assess risk and decide appropriate action despite the fear.

We're born with very few or no fears. Fears are mostly created by parents. The parent who screams and displays panic when their young child trips and falls rarely realizes this misplaced love generates fear and anxiety in the child. Most children fear darkness, strangers, scary creatures and films, and many other irrational things. Living in this fear-infested, frightening world creates unhappiness and unwanted negative thoughts for children, while also suppressing curiosity and courage to try new things, leading to less fun and learning. I know this because I've experienced both being afraid and not being afraid, and the difference in quality of life is staggering.

When I became father to my daughter Evelyn, I learned much about fear and courage. I've never been more worried or scared than when entering the delivery room at the hospital (including matches against eight different world champions). Would my wife be okay? What if my baby isn't healthy and I have to parent a perpetually sick child? What if I can't be a good father? How do you cut an umbilical cord? Thoughts raced and complete helplessness flooded my mind. Meanwhile, my daughter's mother-to-be remained completely calm, focused, and pleasantly excited. Whether from hormones, her self-talk, or a combination, her mental state was perfect. It took all my mental training and discipline to escape the fear state and become useful and supportive. Fortunately, we (she specifically) delivered a wonderful, healthy daughter who has since been my primary positive catalyst for self-talk.

Parenting presents interesting philosophical dilemmas. For example, if you fear ants or, like my friend, have an irrational fear of pigeons (have you noticed how other people's phobias that you don't share always sound ridiculous, while your own seem legitimately scary?), would you teach your child to fear the same things? Most parents would say they don't want to transmit their fears to their children. Yet that's exactly what they do. Through facial expressions, comments, avoiding pigeon-filled squares or ant-covered ground, fears often transmit subconsciously and unnecessarily.

I once interviewed a team of daredevil photographers who accepted the world's most extreme photo missions. Before drones, they were the ones jumping from planes alongside skydivers or skiing off Mont Blanc (yes, someone was actually taking those pictures), performing the same death-defying stunts as their subjects while simultaneously photographing them. I was amazed by their courage and almost childlike fascination with danger rather than terror. They explained they had renamed fear the "performance pulse" and longed for the next opportunity to feel that adrenaline rush build. They had mental models where they felt grateful for such exciting moments and experienced ecstasy rather than fear during adventures.

I recognize the same Mindchange thinking from my fighting experience and from reading accounts of soldiers entering battle, who later miss the front lines when safely home (though PTSD is more common for soldiers). The brain responds to words, and the difference between feeling and saying you're scared versus feeling and saying you're excited matters significantly. When scared, your body reacts with increased blood pressure, dilated pupils, and rapidly pumping heart. The same happens when excited, but instead of locking you down, excitement unlocks your full potential. Try embracing that bubbling stomach feeling and tingling sensation as it builds, feeling grateful to be so alive. You can also take comfort knowing you're never more prepared to perform at your absolute best than in this state.

> *"What would you do if you weren't afraid?"*
>
> Sign at Google headquarters entrance

Hate

For some reason, humans tend to polarize and even hate. From hating math to hating your ex-girlfriend's ridiculous new boyfriend to hating Jews or middle-aged white men. Hate is powerful because it fuels passion almost like love, but unlike love, it's always destructive in both action and thought. Thinking hateful thoughts affects your overall ability to think positively, to love, and to live harmoniously. It also affects you physically (compare Gargamel's sickly appearance to eternally fresh Papa Smurf in Smurfs cartoons for concrete evidence). Physical effects include increased stress hormones like adrenaline and cortisol. Excessive cortisol is toxic for many reasons, from reducing muscle recovery to more systemic problems. The immune system, skin, blood pressure, and numerous other bodily functions are directly or indirectly affected by harboring hate, with absolutely no upside.

The good news is that hate is a chosen emotion, so you can decide not to choose it. Not choosing hate differs from forgiving or accepting wrongdoing—it's a conscious decision to live in a beautiful state rather than a hateful one. Nelson Mandela spent 27 years in prison and emerged without hate. He lived by the Ubuntu philosophy, as President Obama explained at Mandela's memorial service:

"There is a word in South Africa—Ubuntu—a word that captures Mandela's greatest gift: his realization that we are all connected in ways invisible to the eye, that there is a oneness to humanity, that we achieve ourselves by sharing with others and caring for those around us.

We can never know how much of this sense was innate in him, or how much was shaped in a dark, solitary cell. But we remember the gestures big and small—introducing his jailers as honored guests at his inauguration, wearing a Springbok uniform, turning his family's heartbreak into a call to confront HIV/AIDS—that revealed his empathy's depth and his understanding. He not only embodied Ubuntu, he taught millions to find that truth within themselves."

Throughout my life, I've hated almost no one. I came close briefly when a business associate who was my friend and partner greedily abandoned our handshake agreement, claiming we had no contract, then sold the company for tens of millions of euros. Or with romantic rivals in my younger years, or criminals who hurt my friends. Today I hate no one and hope I never will. I also know this is my choice.

My dear friend Felicio taught me a mindset that works for curing hate and preventing random frustrating people from affecting you. Felicio was temporarily obsessed with World of Warcraft, an online game featuring dragons and clan enemies, requiring teamwork amid high stress and heated emotions. He didn't realize the profound wisdom he shared when telling me he never argued with annoying or hateful players. Instead, there was an "ignore" button that, once pressed, made the jerk disappear forever from his world. Fantastic! Rather than wanting to reprimand, punish, or dwell on them, you could press a button and remove them from your game and mind. I've since applied this to every annoying person I've encountered. I politely say hello, treat their words as elevator music that doesn't concern me, and hit the mental ignore button. "Ignore" is far more powerful than retaliation or hate. It reduces the opponent's value and ability to affect you to zero. It also creates something beautiful: if you remain polite and non-confrontational during occasional encounters, there's a chance they'll change over time or circumstances will shift, and you might actually like each other. If not, just keep hitting the ignore button.

Death

We are the only species aware of our inevitable death. This finality is something every human must reconcile with in some way, and failing to do so likely results in existential anguish and death anxiety. As mentioned in the fear section, we're highly irrational in choosing our fears, tending to underestimate real threats while harboring ridiculous phobias. When it comes to death, the situation differs.

For religious practitioners whose faith prescribes continued existence after death, death represents merely a transition to another dimension or life form. This isn't so much fear of death as fear of what that existence will entail. Many religions clearly distinguish between afterlife conditions for the righteous, who will be rewarded in paradise, Nirvana, meet their ancestors, or dine in Odin's halls, versus sinners, who await terrible fates. This can be a strong negative catalyst for anyone feeling sinful. For the righteous, the concept of heaven can beautifully remedy life's terrible hardships, and especially during harsh historical periods, religion has carried humanity through our deepest despair.

Non-believers face a different challenge. For them, developing a peaceful relationship with death and spirituality is essential to avoid the existential anxiety spreading like a pandemic in secular societies, where lack of faith leaves many with a void.

When thinking about death, several truths are typically available to choose from: • Believing in continued existence • Believing life ends completely • Leaving the door open to both possibilities

Personally, I'm rationally inclined to believe death ends my consciousness—there's no soul separate from my body, and I won't experience rebirth, afterlife, or existence in another dimension. Yet I've witnessed many inexplicable wonders during my travels, so I leave a wide door open for new knowledge, perspectives, and potential truths. With Mindchange thinking, I also ask what makes me happiest to believe? In my case, I've decided to view death as the greatest adventure, ready to explore heaven or hell, haunt friends mischievously as a ghost, visit Nangijala, reincarnate as a koala bear, or whatever fate awaits. Just the fact that 4,000 religions claim to know what happens (and all insist everyone else is wrong) makes it a fascinating riddle we'll all solve eventually.

My father, a lifelong atheist, has since becoming paralyzed made a conscious effort to embrace Christianity because his beloved assistants Lemlem and Solomon read him the Bible, and he finds comfort in their message. I stared disbelievingly at his new crucifix necklace and asked what made him religious. He smiled and said: "There are no atheists in the trenches at a war, and I've lived a good life I'm proud of, so it feels good to believe Christianity is real and I'll have a nice continuation in the next life." Whether he created a deliberate delusion or genuinely became a born-again Christian at 90, he passes both the pragmatic and Mindchange tests—it makes him happier.

I'm also a technology optimist and remain open to extended lifespans as technology advances exponentially while costs drop exponentially. The impact of exponential technological development can be illustrated simply: if you walk 30 steps linearly, you end up 30 meters from your starting point. If you walk 30 steps exponentially, doubling the distance each step, you travel 1 billion meters. What would it mean if your smartphone, self-driving car, missile defense system, or generative AI becomes a billion times smarter in 30 years? From this perspective, we begin understanding that concepts that sounded like science fiction just years ago deserve serious consideration, including potentially curing aging and even death.

This thought makes me both excited and calm. Excited about possibilities for increasingly advanced body parts (I already have new eye lenses, two hip replacements, and a new tooth) and charting my path to longevity and health through biohacking and medical innovations. But it also reassures me to recall Bodil Jönsson's words—that I have all the time I need and maybe more.

Combined, my open door to magical life continuation and faith in longevity research buffer me against death anxiety and provide strength and positive thoughts that carry me through others' deaths, even those close to me.

Summary

- Negative catalysts are elements in your life that generate negative thoughts and feelings.
- For many people, past events represent the worst negative catalysts. With Mindchange thinking, you can relate to these events differently, gradually taking charge of your thoughts and feelings even after sad or terrible experiences.
- Negative catalysts can also include destructive relationships, poor health, stress, lack of love, meaning, and confidence, among others.
- How you view time, aging, and your progress in life can be powerful negative catalysts. Understanding that even time is a human invention allows you, through Mindchange thinking, to develop a relationship with time and aging that makes you curious and happy. As Bodil Jönsson says, we all have plenty of time.
- Finding a harmonious relationship with death is crucial. It makes coping with others' deaths easier—a major source of unhappiness for most people. It also makes contemplating your own death and what follows less frightening and perhaps even exciting.

Living a Good Life

BY NOW YOU probably have a good understanding of Mindchange thinking. You've likely reflected on your own "default setting" or starting point for taking command of your inner voice and making it the love of your life. Perhaps you've begun identifying your positive and negative catalysts and considering how you want to maintain, change, or reconsider your view of them. With these insights and hopefully a healthy dose of curiosity, let's explore what a good life looks like and what it means (for you) to live one.

For me, the highest level of thinking—or if you prefer, the meaning of life—is to live a good life with happiness both short and long-term, with the ability to interpret whatever happens in a way that keeps me harmonious. Living a happy life therefore revolves around how you talk to yourself and how your inner voice becomes your best, kindest, wisest, and most supportive companion through life.

In practice, this can mean being happy with your past, even if parts of it were awful. It means being happy and excited about the future, knowing that your interpretation matters more than what actually happens—as my daughter said when she was seven: "The most exciting thing in the universe is the future." But it's also about effectively removing and rethinking negative catalysts, freeing up mental space for more joyful thoughts and actions.

It's about understanding and developing your positive catalysts—or as my friend Niklas put it, "Happiness is doing less of what you don't like and more of what you do like"—simple but powerful words. Then you can build your own meaningful story and make it passionate, understanding the intimate relationship between doing something passionately and actually creating the feeling of passion through doing, which ultimately creates purpose.

There are no required conditions or universal blueprints. You can be the world's happiest person without ever having children, having sex, having a country, or winning the lottery (ask the Dalai Lama). In my view, the definition of living a good life must be personal, although certain choices seem to consistently make it easier or harder to live happily ever after, as shown in the sections on catalysts. Rather than telling you how to think, in the next section I'll share my personal roadmap in hopes it might guide or at least inspire you to develop your own.

Before reading the next chapter, consider: What is a good life for you?

My Personal Story and My Mantras

How I Talk to Myself

AFTER SEVERAL DECADES of speaking well to myself, I've created a loving, fun, and extremely respectful yet playful relationship with myself. I write "respectful" because respect represents a crucial quality when talking to yourself. For example, I never, ever speak rudely to myself or say mean, critical things in my inner dialogue. If I miss a flight, I don't hear my inner voice saying "you fucking idiot, you can never get anything right" but rather "missed flights happen to the best of us, and hey Ola, it just did. What can we do for fun here at the airport, or how can we play the ball from here?" I usually add a mental pat on the shoulder because in that moment, I feel I'm handling an unfortunate situation exceptionally well.

I also frequently remind myself that I'm special and wonderful (perhaps not objectively true, but in that case, it's a purposeful delusion for me) which gives me comfort and the feeling that things will work out.

I'm also deeply anchored in the belief that the only thing determining my happiness and harmony is how I talk to myself. This gives me both the right and the obligation to direct my thoughts and feelings so they serve my purpose—having an amazing, happy life based on my personal definition of what's happy and amazing.

Positive Catalysts

"If you see a doctor who gives you medicine before you've eaten, exercised, and slept properly, he's not a doctor, but a drug dealer."

Dr. Ivan Rusiliko

Health and Well-being

I understand my health represents an important positive catalyst and therefore dedicate time to it. I also feel pride in being healthy. I allow myself to be proud of my championship medals, my toned abs, and my ability to dance all night without tiring. I do this much like an academic takes pride in their knowledge and titles, without spending much time worrying about others' opinions.

Exercise

Regarding health, I've continuously created sporting challenges that push me to train and maintain good fitness. When facing the prospect of world-class fighters soon trying to kick and punch you in the face, it becomes natural to hit the gym and train as hard as possible. This explains why I've made continuous comebacks and, in the past decade, won medals in 6 Swedish taekwondo championships (gold, silver, and bronze), represented Sweden in two European and one World Championships (not in my age category, but against the world's best), and won two Swedish Championships gold medals in All Styles (stand-up MMA rules).

This year, as mentioned, I've embarked on my latest martial arts career and won kickboxing European championship and

World Cup gold medals in the 40+ category, but also international competitions against 20-year-old champions. Even without competitions, I've gamified my training by giving myself points when I work out or creating other elements that make training fun. For example, I've vowed to only watch my favorite shows while on the treadmill or to take hour-long walks at airports before flights, and I've scheduled training sessions instead of business dinners to make exercise a constant part of my life.

Another hack is EMS training using a suit that delivers electrical impulses to muscles, making 20 minutes of intense EMS training equivalent to 2-3 hours in the gym. I always travel with this suit—it's been a game-changer for me. On days when I can't work out, I use an app with a 10-minute routine that I do twice, which has been a great "workout for days when I don't have time to workout" hack.

I have many friends where our typical social interaction involves exercise, which makes staying fit easier. Exercise represents one of my main positive catalysts because it provides endorphins, calmness, strength, and a good feeling in my body—all making it easier to speak well to myself.

Sleep

I try to sleep 8 hours daily and regularly have extended sleep sessions where I often sleep up to 12 hours (after jet lag, partying, or just starting a vacation). My circadian rhythm—when I'm genetically programmed to sleep and wake—is 1:55 AM to 9:55 AM with a 40-minute nap some days. Since modern work life follows a different rhythm, and I live alone with my daughter who wants breakfast at 7 AM before school, this initially created a problem as I always went to bed well after midnight anyway.

I restructured my work to allow an extra hour of sleep after dropping her off, and now my sleep pattern is perfect (I know because my Oura ring measures sleep quality nightly). I also schedule sleep-in mornings into my work calendar and during certain weekends, especially when living in Ibiza part of the year or visiting destinations with late nights that would otherwise take their toll.

Peace of Mind

I've practiced traditional karate since childhood, and in this tradition, meditation begins and ends every session, so finding a quiet mental space comes naturally to me. I also use simple meditation techniques like slowly scanning each body part and/or counting breaths. I've developed a mental destination—a place or sanctuary where I can go and completely disconnect from surrounding distractions, even during a dentist's tooth extraction (which happened a few weeks ago) or other disruptions.

Try finding this place by imagining yourself harmoniously content somewhere—perhaps in nature, your childhood bedroom, or at sea—wherever makes you feel calm. Then develop the imagery, adding beautiful calming elements until your mental paradise perfectly suits you. Control your breathing with deep, calm inhalations and exhalations while sitting comfortably. Start by counting breaths while visualizing a river where thoughts flow past without stopping, until fewer thoughts appear and finally you're present without thinking. Then enter your mental paradise. Try it—it's more enjoyable than a dental appointment.

Karate also teaches breathing techniques, such as in Sanshin kata and Tensho, that combine muscle tension and relaxation. Similar exercises are now fashionable, with breathing studios teaching what's now trendily called "breathwork."

I also own a wonderful meditation gadget—a headband called Muse that creates soundscapes, like a beach environment, while monitoring my brainwaves during meditation. If my brain shifts to the wrong frequencies and stress begins, it changes the weather sounds or wave noises until I control my thoughts and regain mental calm. This has taught me how my brain works and what I can do to achieve a calm mental state in seconds.

For me, peace of mind also means having alone time—periods for myself where I can reflect, read, or think. TTT: Thinking Takes Time. During these sessions, I feel I develop my Mindchange thinking most significantly.

Having fun!

"Creativity is intelligence having fun."

Albert Einstein

As mentioned earlier, I take fun very seriously and believe I plan and create playful events more than most people. These might be elaborate children's parties for Evelyn and 80 friends based on Burning Man principles, or adult gatherings in Mykonos or Ibiza. I've had more fun at night than during daytime and spent more hours on dance floors than in front of televisions. I also try bringing a culture of fun to companies I'm involved with, like our innovation house Epicenter offering microchip implants instead of office keys, allowing staff to attend as remote-controlled robots, or hosting alcohol-free raves after hours.

I dye my hair blue when Evelyn requests it and have picked her up from school in a kung fu panda costume (unfortunately, some adults thought I was a school shooter). We also held a "mandatory masquerade day" at one of my companies but only informed our CFO, who arrived dressed as a chicken and looked utterly bewildered when he was the only one in costume. I highly value playfulness in the people I spend most time with and have wonderful, crazy friends who are magicians, DJs, philosophers, performance artists, and brilliant thinkers. This is partly because playful people attract each other, but it was also a conscious strategy to live the life I want, as many age-peers began deprioritizing the playfulness I value so highly and instead (with no judgment of others' choices) started behaving like typical adults their age, discussing old fun memories more than creating new ones.

For me, as described above, Nevada's desert and Burning Man represented a playfulness and fun Mecca. Einstein said creativity is intelligence having fun, and this manifests in countless ways during the amazing desert experiences. If you're inspired by this and want to introduce more playfulness into your life and among friends, start by planning some unusual activities and events that you find fun and bring everyone along. Also, consider who makes you laugh most and ensure you see them frequently. Similarly with activities you enjoy—if you find stand-up comedy fun, buy tickets for yourself and friends.

Love

I believe a major societal problem is that many people in relationships are unhappy and often long for something outside the relationship or believe the grass is greener elsewhere. Meanwhile, most singles I know worry about not finding "the one," and if they don't have children yet, this might cause additional stress. I think this "not happy in relationships" and "not happy when single" problem creates significant negative thoughts individually, between couples, and societally. I continuously apply Mindchange thinking to be happy whether in relationships or single. I loved my wife completely and was the world's happiest man when we married and committed to spending our lives together.

Now I'm very happy being single and can focus entirely on making my daughter's life wonderful (which doesn't mean spoiling her except with love, experiences, and wisdom). I also have opportunities to meet fascinating women as dates, friends, lovers, and perhaps someday my soul mate. What's not to like? As you now understand, this epitomizes Mindchange thinking. Your condition doesn't determine your happiness—you do. To facilitate this, I've created a new love map outlining what I truly want now in a partner, which I believe will guide my love adventures. I also have wonderful female friends who are constant parts of Evelyn's and my life, for which I'm deeply grateful—you know who you are. Armed with my love map, a core of strong, fun female friends, flirtatious adventures, and my life experience so far, I'm excited to see how my love life unfolds in the next exciting chapter—a thought that gives me endorphins and goosebumps.

SEX!

As mentioned earlier, this isn't a book about my sex life, which I prefer keeping private. However, I want to share some lessons learned, primarily about attitudes toward sex. Sex as a concept can be a source of feverish desire, guilt, betrayal, risk, children, disease, and much more—but also one of the most connected, exciting, and beautiful experiences humans can share. Thinking, saying, and doing things in alignment has been an important guiding principle helping me live authentically according to my hopes and desires. I challenge you, dear reader, to do the same and let YOUR thoughts and actions be guided by yourself rather than conventions, fears, parents, culture, or concerns about gossip. Sex can be a continuous source of feeling alive and experiencing real happiness—don't miss the opportunity (my phone number is +46... just kidding).

Love for My Daughter

All parents understand, but few non-parents do. The love I feel for Evelyn resembles first love at school, or loving your favorite team winning championships, or seeing your idol in concert for the first time. Simultaneously, it lacks grandiosity and bombast. Watching your child taste a lemon for the first time or point at a car and say "lamp" or something similar makes your day complete. My positive catalyst and chosen truth is that the more time I spend with Evelyn, the happier she and I become. I take Evelyn with me whenever possible, and she's visited every continent. She's dived the Great Barrier Reef, celebrated New Year in Tokyo, hung out with movie stars and graffiti artists in LA, rappelled through rainforests, slept in Delhi taxi parks, swam with whales in Maui, visited a Tulum nightclub (claiming she was a little person, not a child, and demanding the doorman show respect), and has her own Star Alliance gold card for air travel.

Traveling and experiencing together is "our thing." In my professional life, I traveled several times weekly for 20 years and lived "everywhere all the time," as a friend described it. Showing her my world and seeing it through a child's eyes represents one of my greatest joys. I recognize that what I do for and with her isn't possible for many (and perhaps not even interesting or desirable), but it works for us, and I've worked hard and built relationships worldwide to give her keys to the world's mysteries. It's not primarily about money or fancy trips—it's about father-daughter time and shared dreams we realize and remember forever.

I also value our ongoing, often philosophical discussions, which for me are frequently more interesting and challenging than small talk with adults. My way of giving love and friendship to both adults and children is sharing and teaching things I've learned that might benefit them. Sometimes I'm misunderstood as wanting to appear knowledgeable or all-knowing, but that's never my intention. When you begin mastering Mindchange thinking, you feel an almost irresistible urge to share it with others to alleviate their problems, rather than discussing the problem itself, which can frustrate friends or partners. With my daughter, this is never an issue because I created her "default setting," and my paternal responsibility and highest ambition is being her guide through the journey to a good life. My advice to non-parents is to care for a child—your own or someone else's—and "do" parenting because it's an empowering, self-propelling source of happiness and indeed a verb.

Family

I have a very small family. My father who at this writing is 91 and paralyzed (but happy—see the appendix interview to learn why), my 88-year-old mother (who isn't as happy despite having everything, having never embraced Mindchange thinking), my brother Jens and his family with girlfriend Bella and children Lodin (my daughter's best friend) and Wynja (a younger version of my daughter). That's all of us. I've decided my family is my fortress and I'm always there for them, just as they've been for me. It's always been this way because I'm fortunate to have had an amazing, loving family.

Now I've experienced a phase where we children change roles from being cared for, supported, and confided in by our parents to becoming increasingly their caretakers, to them recently becoming quite dependent on us. Mindchange has helped me not only shoulder this responsibility but also feel pride and joy in doing so. The role of being their knight in shining armor solving problems and creating wonderful experiences (like flying my paralyzed father to Athens and Mykonos because he always wanted to see Greece, or helping him publish his memoirs) has given me purpose despite objectively difficult, sad circumstances.

Making my brother and his children close friends with my daughter and me through shared memories and values has been a priority, and I'd rather travel with them to places they enjoy than visit destinations that are more adult-oriented and my preference. All these are choices based on truths about family and my self-image of who I want to be as son, brother, uncle, and father. The beautiful thing is that when you truly "do" family passionately, you become passionate about family, and it becomes a powerful positive catalyst.

Avoiding Negative Catalysts

Among the worst negative catalysts, as mentioned earlier, are unhealthy lifestyles and abusing anything from drugs to alcohol to poor food choices. Overcoming these negative behaviors is relatively straightforward in terms of knowing what to do. The difficulty lies in actually changing the behavior.

I've always enjoyed partying, and occasionally I meet people (old friends, acquaintances) with distorted views of my lifestyle, some even expressing loving concern I might die a rock star death from sex, drugs, and rock 'n' roll. While I don't completely rule this out, I must admit I have very clear controls and boundaries against excesses. I've been on national teams or at the highest sporting level for most of my life. I'm also subject to continuous anti-doping testing for steroids, drugs, etc., so I can scientifically prove I live a very healthy life overall.

This represents a chosen strategy because pursuing maximum fun without health considerations eventually creates terrible negative catalysts. People who begin consuming too much alcohol, drugs, or even sex will sooner or later find themselves consumed by these activities. In my case, I've always been able to establish rules—for example, no more than the recommended maximum 14 alcohol units weekly. Or making September alcohol-free every year. Or no partying two months before a fight. Or no hard liquor this year. This gamification tactic has saved me from myself during intense periods of business dinners every night or new guests arriving weekly at my Ibiza house for "crazy party weeks," which represent one week for them but eight consecutive weeks that summer for me, making it important I don't maintain their pace. This strategy has also allowed me to occasionally party hard without negative consequences (beyond wallet damage and a few missing brain cells).

Avoid Drama

Regarding relationships, a very small number of relationships probably bring you the most negativity and frustration. Destructive relationships often represent a dominant unhappiness source, and understanding this and avoiding or changing them can provide a shortcut to happiness. For me, there's a simple truth: you know if a relationship is bad or good for you. Let that sink in. You DO know! If still uncertain, ask yourself: Would you want your child to marry the person you're with? If not, why not? That's why you shouldn't be with them either. Period.

Mantras and Useful Spells

The word "mantra" comes from Hindu tradition and describes a word given by a master to disciples as a meditation focus through repetition. Western culture has since adopted it with the meaning "repeated statement or phrase." In the Mindchange model, I use "mantra" or "spell" interchangeably for sentences that provide positive energy and help me think correctly. Like Hindu mantras, you need to repeat them so they gradually become part of you and naturally guide and protect you through life. I prefer "spell" because it suggests power and magic in words but also connects to spelling—you need to articulate the words and spell them with your inner voice.

Below I share some of my most important mantras or spells that I tell myself, that are true for me, and have served me well. I hope you can adopt and use some to direct your thinking in different situations.

I am never negative or rude to myself - this thought ensures I always treat myself kindly. My thought experiment is always being at least as loving to myself as to my daughter.

What's the worst that can happen - this cures much unnecessary worry, fear, and hesitation. If I'm not afraid or worried about the worst-case scenario, I can focus my energy on the task rather than worrying. In 90% of cases, the worst outcome isn't that difficult—

riding a roller coaster, asking someone to dance, attending a job interview, or trying to write a happiness-promoting book. However, sometimes this mantra also protects me from wrong choices because the worst is too serious to risk.

The world is getting better and better - there are so many beautiful developments happening every second and minute worldwide, and I've decided to focus on these rather than media doom and gloom. In my chosen truth, both I and the world are healthier, wealthier, safer, and wiser than ever before, and I feel immense gratitude to be alive now, probably the best time in human existence.

Laziness never affects my decision to do something for or with my daughter - I'm never lazy as in "I'm too tired to do this with or for Evelyn." If I feel that's why I don't want to drive her to soccer practice or go back looking for her ski pole on the slope or help with homework, this spell activates and makes me "just f*cking do it!" I sometimes hear Sensei's words "Gambate Ola-san" (gambate means do your best in Japanese) giving me the energy boost needed to do what's right. Having made this self-promise actually makes parenting much easier. A necessary life hack for a single dad with commitments to 12 businesses, a sports career, and numerous fun social events.

Win or learn - UFC megastar Conor McGregor says he can't lose. He either wins or learns from defeat, which isn't losing but evolving. This resonated deeply with me and helped me stop worrying about lost fights or other failures. For a long time now, the spell appears in my head saying (almost with Conor's Irish accent): You win or you learn! What did you learn this time?

Death is the greatest adventure. How exciting! - I described my views on death and longevity in the Death section. In extremely scary situations like cockpit fires requiring emergency landings, lightning striking another plane during landing, or facing eight different world champions under various full-contact rules—this reassures me by viewing death as the greatest adventure.

The smarter someone is, the more they like me - I typically use this spell when someone seems to dislike or misunderstand me, which happens occasionally, probably because I do many things in many areas and am therefore harder to categorize in ways that make sense. As this statement demonstrates, your spells don't need to be factually true or even sensible to others. In this case, it's nicer to think of someone who doesn't understand me as someone who would if they were smarter or had more information. It's also a tribute to people who like me—people I obviously admire for their intelligence and remarkable ability to judge character :).

Every year gets better - I don't fear aging and believe technological medical advances will do wonders for the aging population's living conditions. It's conceivable we'll be stronger (through exoskeletons, for example), happier, have better sex lives, learn more, and dance as much at 70 as at 20. I actually enjoy life more every year. This involves several factors and positive catalysts: having freedom and means to design my life, but also another year developing my inner voice to keep me happy and excited. The fact that Evelyn is growing and our conversations and adventures are evolving also makes each year a pleasure, and I look forward to next year's end when my new titanium hip has learned enough kickboxing to win the World Championships again.

Impossible is just an opinion without empirical evidence - this powerful quote comes from Google founder Larry Page. I spent a week at the World Economic Forum in Davos for three consecutive years, and the Google founders were also there since we'd all been elected as Global Leaders of Tomorrow. I remember people thought they were copycats trying to replicate Yahoo, the leading search engine then, and didn't seem very innovative. They truly became global leaders, while I did not (I'm happy for them and genuinely impressed, but wouldn't change or alter my life because I'm so romantically in love with the journey I've made and will continue). We thought they were on a suicide mission copying Yahoo. In reality, they changed the world for everyone and forever became two of history's richest and most important people. Impossible is just an opinion without empirical evidence. I use this to energize myself when odds are against me, like fighting world champions or when ideas or businesses seem hopeless based on conventional wisdom.

I am special and wonderful - I'll try explaining this very un-Swedish self-perception by describing what I mean by each word. I am special in that many statistics or generalized truths about men my age are based on people who don't live, think, or do what I do. My physique and health differ, my hip surgery recovery was ten times faster than expected, and my reaction time exceeded 40% of all national team men despite being well over 40. The companies I've started have operated differently and unusually, whether starting the horse game Starstable.com focusing on games for girls rather than boys, the innovation house Epicenter focusing on community members' needs rather than maximizing square footage rentals through long contracts, or buying a Miami house when everyone feared the worst crisis ever (the house has increased sixfold in value over 14 years). I try doing things my way without being influenced by conventions. This sentence helps me remember and develop my uniqueness. The second part, "I am wonderful," makes me less concerned about being different, odd, or wrong because I think being different and thinking and doing things differently is wonderful. It also gives me positive endorphins. Try it yourself. Say "I am wonderful" and focus on the feeling.

I have many other spells in my repertoire that help with everything from feeling like I'm having a good hair day when public opinion suggests otherwise, to powerful phrases getting me to the gym or working out intensely once there, to being a good son or loyal partner. On mindchanged.com, I've shared a link to my mantras and those of many readers. Please use what you find meaningful and upload your wisest spells to inspire others.

Summary

This chapter is meant to inspire you to start using the Mindchange model yourself.

Think about what you can do to improve your:

• health • sleep • diet • peace of mind

Feel free to write down your ideas or, better yet, schedule them. What do you find fun? Try planning four fun activities as if they were your most important meetings.

Which friends and social situations give you the most positive energy? Do you see those friends enough? Try texting them right now to express your appreciation and suggest meeting to do things you enjoy.

Think about love—feel free to complete your Love Map using the template at the book's end and on Mindchanged.com.

Look at the different love concepts below and dream about

how you could experience each or consider a real person with whom you share respective types of love:

Agape - Unconditional love Eros - Romantic love Philia - Friendly love Storge - Family love Ludus - Playful love Mania - Obsession Pragma - Enduring love Philautia - Self-love

Mantras or spells are powerful incantations making it easier to speak well to yourself and gain energy. Try applying my mantras to situations in your life:

"I am never negative or rude to myself" "What is the worst that can happen" "The world is getting better and better" "Laziness never affects my decision to do something for or with my daughter" "I win or I learn" "Death is the greatest adventure. So exciting!" "The smarter someone is, the more they like me" "Every year gets better" "Impossible is just an opinion without empirical evidence" "I am special and wonderful"

The World Needs a New Narrative

I HOPE THAT you have enjoyed reading this book and that you have realized that far fewer things are set in stone than many people believe. Most aspects of our lives are human creations, and we can change them in our own minds and in society as a whole. YOU own your story and are the author of your own life and happiness.

I've written this book because I want to be a positive catalyst for your happiness and that of many others, but also because the world needs a new story, a new unifying cry that isn't a battle cry, and a smarter, more conscious way to live happily ever after.

Imagine a world where all children grow up mastering their emotions and living without fear, self-loathing, or worry. Imagine a world where most people feel joy and purpose instead of taking pills to combat the growing epidemic of meaninglessness. Imagine political and business leaders looking beyond profits and power structures to co-create a sustainable society that makes it easier for more people to live happy, fulfilled lives. What if that sad, bullied school shooter had mastered Mindchange thinking instead of creating the internal narratives that killed innocent children? What if Putin took more pride in his ability to create harmony and not react to provocations than in his nationalist and historical will to power?

What kind of higher levels of thinking and emotion will we need to master an AI with far greater logical intelligence than our own? Perhaps some answers lie in Mindchange thinking.

I certainly don't have all the answers, but I'm pretty confident that we need a revolution in thinking that will allow more people of all ages, religions, and nationalities to think better and succeed in their pursuit of happy, fulfilled lives. I hope that the journey that brought you to read this book will continue and that you also have the opportunity (even a responsibility) to share your learnings with others. When people feel good, they generally treat others better, and the ripples from a positive thought revolution could be enormous.

Is this the naïve dream of a middle-aged Swedish wannabe writer? Maybe so, but I'm convinced of the opposite and believe in our collective ability to embrace important issues. In less than 30 years, a niche weightlifting sport transformed into a global gym and health trend, and now everyone has some relationship with fitness and exercise. Jesus and his disciples helped billions find meaning by following ten simple rules and finding hope even in the most hopeless situations. The vegetarian and plant-based movement has evolved from a few hippies to fundamentally changing global diets. The climate change and sustainability movement has grown from a handful of scientists and environmental activists to influencing every ambitious government and consumer decision worldwide. My conclusion is that YES, it can be done—we CAN collectively create a better story for the world just as you can create a better story for yourself, one thought at a time.

I am writing MY conclusion because this is my chosen truth, and as you now understand, I am the author not only of this book but also of my own thoughts and life story. And so are you...

Extras, Models and Interviews

What Can You Do NOW?

The following pages present simple exercises to deepen your Mindchange journey. None will take more than 10 minutes of your time. All have the potential to forever change any reader's life.

Evaluate Your Default Setting

Below is a section of easy-to-use templates that assess your default setting and break down how you think and feel today into categories you can keep, discard, or develop.

Happiness baseline - how happy are you on a scale of 1-10 (not this very second but rather during this period of your life).

Think about what could make you happier in the short or long term. What are your chosen truths? What thoughts should you stop thinking? Which truths should you choose?

Think about and rate the following factors between 1-10 in terms of how they affect your happiness:

- Your genetics - are you naturally sad or naturally happy or somewhere in between? Put a number between 1-10

- Growing up - does your childhood make you sad or happy, 1-10

- Beliefs and spirituality - does your belief, spirituality or general view of life's big questions make you depressed or happier, 1-10

- Cultural truths - do you feel your culture and values limit or enhance your happiness, 1-10

- Past experiences - do you have bad events that drag down your happiness or good memories that strengthen you, 1-10

- Just by completing this simple exercise, you can begin realizing you can own your narrative and start evolving your default setting.

Think about it and write it down:

- Negative catalysts - what gives you the most negative energy, thoughts, and problems

- Positive catalysts - what brings you the most happiness, positive thoughts and feelings, and flow

- Chosen truths - which chosen truths give you the most negative emotions? Which chosen truths bring you the most happiness?

Look carefully at the list. Do you really need to allow negative catalysts to occupy space in your life? Can you eliminate them? Can you change your attitude toward them?

Look equally closely at your positive catalysts. Can you do more of what you enjoy? (Feel free to schedule these activities in your calendar now to make room for them.)

Can you challenge the negative chosen truths making you unhappy? I hope this anecdote can inspire you: a man moved to Sweden from a poorer country where he had always dreamed of wealth and believed that becoming rich would eliminate all his worries and make him the world's happiest man. His success symbol was driving his dream sports car. Once in Sweden, he earned ten times more than in his home country but still felt poorer than anyone with more. Later, he borrowed his dream sports car for a month and was overjoyed the first day, happy the entire first week, annoyed at all the garage expenses the second week, and let it sit unused the final two weeks.

After just one month of Mindchange thinking, he realized the car wasn't what he truly wanted, nor was it wealth, but rather the security and social status he thought money provided. Looking at his life—rich in friends, love, meaning, and positive catalysts—it became easy to reject his old chosen truth about sports cars and wealth, or as he put it, "the wealth that doesn't need a garage."

Immunity to Change

Harvard psychologist Robert Kegan's model for countering what he calls "Immunity to change" is a complete system requiring a trained moderator and therefore can't be fully done justice in this book.

However, I want to inspire you to consider the model's main questions:

1. What is the most important positive change you could make to improve your life and happiness?

2. What are you doing instead of creating this change (behaviors and thoughts taking you away from the change you want)?

3. How would you feel if you had to change what you're doing instead of creating the change you really want?

4. What chosen truths underpin this thinking?

5. What are your deeply held beliefs?

6. What could you do to change your inner voice to reach your goals as described in the first question?

Translated into a concrete example:

1. I really want to lose weight.

2. Instead, I make jokes about fitness enthusiasts, forget to get a gym membership, always buy snacks for me and the kids, and feel uncomfortable when I do exercise.

3. If I were to change these thoughts and behaviors and take exercise seriously, buy a gym membership, and stop buying sweets, life would feel boring and filled with obligations. I get uneasy just thinking about it.

4. My chosen truth is that it's more boring to be disciplined and that you're uncomfortable if you take exercise seriously.

5. My deeply held belief is that there are bon vivants and then there are those disciplined people, and I don't want to be one of them.

6. I could test whether this is true by exercising with peers who I think enjoy life, thereby changing my core beliefs, which would then change my behavior and help me implement the desired change.

Although this example doesn't do the model justice, it illustrates the underlying, often unknown reasons why people struggle to change their behavior even when they genuinely want to. For me, the model has been a lifelong companion since I had the honor of studying with Kegan.

Please take ten minutes to think about what this process would look like for you.

Your Spells and Mantras

Mantras or spells are powerful incantations that make it easier to speak well to yourself and get energized. Write down mantras you tell yourself that drive your actions, thoughts, and feelings in the right direction.

Visit the Spells Mindchange archive at www.Mindchanged.com where you can explore my mantras and those from other readers that may be useful.

Try applying some of my mantras to situations in your life and notice how they feel:

"I am never negative or rude to myself" "What is the worst that can happen" "The world is getting better and better" "Laziness never affects my decision to do something for or with my daughter" "I win or I learn" "Death is the greatest adventure. So exciting!" "The smarter someone is, the more they like me" "Every year gets better" "Impossible is just an opinion without empirical evidence" "I am special and wonderful"

Create Your Love Map

Here you'll find a simple guide and template to understand what you need, want, and like—and the opposite—when it comes to romantic love, plus a nudge to look in the mirror and see if you can help luck find your right match.

Start by writing down the values, behaviors, and character traits you truly love and want your life partner to embody. Write those under heading 1. Then write down qualities you like but aren't enough to win your heart, and if missing, aren't dealbreakers. Put those under heading 2. Under heading 3, write things you find charming and fun but aren't necessary.

Now do the opposite—write down characteristics that disqualify a potential partner under heading 1. Under heading 2, write things you find unattractive and completely wrong but might tolerate. Under heading 3, write down annoying traits, behaviors, and phenomena you don't like but can accept if everything else balances out.

Be honest; write more rather than fewer items in each section.

Once you've completed both tasks, take a few minutes to consider how your previous partners would appear in this model. Did they possess what you truly need, or did they have several characteristics you don't want in your love life? For me, this was an overwhelming realization because I discovered none of my previous relationships reflected what I really wanted.

The last and often most important step is reflecting on your own behavior and how you'd like to improve and change to become the best possible life partner. Note that these should be changes YOU want to make, not forced or pretended changes.

What I wrote on those six pages when creating my first Love Map is what prepared me to find love, have a child, and live happily ever after.

Love Map

1. Required values, traits and behaviors
2. Desirable values, traits and behaviors
3. Appreciated values, traits and behaviors

VS

1. Not acceptable values, character traits and behaviors
2. Disliked values, traits and behaviors
3. Irritating traits and behaviors

How I Want to Change Myself to Find My Life Partner More Easily

• I have to... • I should think about... • I'm going to do more of...
• I'm going to do less of... • Write free text and set intentions

Sensei – Your Mindchange AI

At mindchanged.com you can chat with Sensei, this book's very own AI agent, who can answer all your questions about

Mindchange thinking and serve as a sounding board for your thoughts. Sensei will continuously evolve and improve at helping you on your Mindchange journey. Remember that it's only an AI and doesn't possess the same wisdom as my real, human Sensei.

Interviews

DURING MY JOURNEY with Mindchange, I've met several people who have mastered Mindchange thinking on their own and who have inspired me during my work. You can get to know some of them here in interview form.

Lars Ahlvarsson, Former Mayor, Chief Negotiator and Hockey Star

My father Lars Ahlvarsson was born in 1933 and grew up during World War II with an unemployed father and mother who did odd jobs and rented out the kitchen sofa in their one-room apartment before things improved. He then had a phenomenal career in public service, serving as both a Stockholm mayor and a member of the Supreme Labor Court, in addition to many board positions, chief negotiator, and mediator roles. Six years ago, he fell and became paralyzed from the neck down with only limited mobility in his limbs, and since then has been unable to walk, eat, or manage hygiene without 24/7 assistance.

What did you think when you realized you were paralyzed, probably forever?

It is of course a very tough situation to be in. The fact that the family was so close and was there for me and did not see me as handicapped or as the Swedish word invalid was very important. I then decided to find all possible solutions and try them and if it still didn't work become the best possible patient.

And he did, and many are the nurses and assistants who over the past six years have become his friends and close allies who laugh and learn and feel greatly appreciated while helping him through the day. The mental strength of "wanting to be the best patient ever" as a vision where few other dreams were within reach made a deep impression on me dealing with my own grief over my dad being paralyzed.

You often say "it's not how you have it but how you take it." What do you mean by that?

Most of what happens in life depends on an external factor. Someone else does something, something happens on a larger scale, someone puts a banana peel on the floor... You can't control every event or action but you can very much influence how you react to it and how you think and feel about it. This skill becomes even more important with every moment, from being lifted and carried to go to the toilet to not being able to scratch your nose and its itch in the middle of the night to not being able to be with family and loved ones. I chose none of this. I can choose how I react to it and I can try to choose to live in a beautiful state rather than a suffering state.

What makes you happy?

It comes in many dimensions. Winning a hockey game and playing at your best (my dad was an elite hockey player in the top division for AIK). Or having the memory of that win and being proud.

I am also very proud of my career and what I have achieved. Who would have thought that a high school dropout with a reputation for being a troublemaker would become a mayor of the nation's capital? I think an important part of happiness is looking back on a life that you are proud of and that makes you happy when you look back.

I am also proud of my sons' achievements and my long and

harmonious relationship with my wife, who has been my closest ally since we met in primary school. I also receive a lot of kindness and love from the people who take care of me, especially some of those who have become like daughters and sons to me.

My family has been a strength. It was always nice to come home.

Most parents are afraid that something will happen to their sons. I've had more than 200 fights and faced 8 world champions in several different martial arts. You have not seemed to be very worried. My brother Jens was a soldier in Lebanon with the UN peacekeeping forces and you didn't worry much either. What do you think about this (asking for a friend)?

I've probably worried a bit, but not in a way that bothers me or is a big part of parenting. Maybe it's because I've taken so many hits in so many ways that I know what a strong person can take and still keep standing up.

You also want to say yes to life and its opportunities. What do you mean by this?

I have always said yes to opportunities and challenges and had confidence that I will find a way to solve them. After a while, you have taken a chance and won so many times that it builds up confidence and you are also in a position where you can afford to make a mistake without ruining your future opportunities.

An attitude of saying yes and seeing what happens makes life so much more interesting. Challenging at times but also much more rewarding.

Where did this self-confidence come from?

I always played with the older guys and I learnt a lot from

them. Both good things and some not so good. It made me develop faster and I became hardened in a tougher environment. It made me believe in my own ability and taught me how to come back if I failed.

As for my own sense of worth, it comes from something completely different. My father, your grandfather. He was in many ways a hard man and tough on me, both as a strategy and because that's how children were brought up in the 30s and 40s. Boys don't cry and you get a slap in the face if you respond in the wrong way. I can honestly say it never bothered me because he also had a strong sense of fair play and I probably needed a firm hand sometimes.

What really made me feel important and loved for being me was how he was always there for me when I was training or playing important matches. He was literally at every football match, which is important for a young kid... If there was only one spectator at the match and 10 minus outside, I didn't have to look who it was. I knew it was my dad. I felt appreciated.

Do you think there is a genetic component to building a strong psyche?

I think genetics makes it more or less difficult to learn the right lessons. Like in your case with Sensei. You had the receptivity and the cognitive abilities to accept and learn from Sensei's teachings. I also learnt a lot from him. Especially when it came to you and when to keep you on a short leash to keep you safe and when to let you roam free to develop.

You are very kind and considerate to others, why and how do you think about kindness?

It's simple: if I don't want someone to do a certain thing to me, I wouldn't do it to anyone else. Moreover, I would not let anyone else do it either. This integrity of not backing down has been a guiding strategy for me.

What do you want to see in future leaders?

Leaders must understand politics, leadership and society. It is also important to understand that they can never lie, not even a white lie. A leader must show the way, must lead. That doesn't mean you can't ask others for advice, but you have to take the final decision, the responsibility and lead by example from the front line.

What is your view on religion and the existence of a higher power than us?

I have spent most of my life as an ardent atheist. But recently, I have opened the door to a more spiritual worldview. Spirituality and a sense of divine presence has been both a conscious choice given my situation or as they say, there are no atheists in the trenches, but it has also gradually grown on me. I felt something was missing and believed that faith had many of the answers. And I don't mean ceremonies and priests running around, but rather the deep togetherness and common understanding of what is important and values. I went deeper and found a spirituality and a like-minded flow of thoughts and feelings. I expected to be criticised by people around me and was prepared for it, but it did not happen.

What happens after death?

To quote Henry Kissinger: "Surprise me!"

Evelyn Gray

I felt it was both fun and important to share the thoughts of Evelyn Gray Ahlvarsson, my daughter who, at the age of 8, started giving speeches about courage and how parents should raise courageous children.

My daughter, like many children, often says funny, interesting and thought-provoking things, and I sometimes post them on Instagram or Facebook. One sentence she said was "children can only learn fear from the faces of their parents and children who are afraid become the parents of afraid children and create a world where they live in fear." A conference organizer contacted me, and I assumed he wanted to book me as a speaker, but he actually wanted Evelyn on stage. She accepted the challenge, and we rehearsed a ten-minute speech which she delivered brilliantly, leading to more bookings (you can see her on YouTube by searching "Evelyn Gray talks about courage." You can also book her, but she doesn't haggle on her fees: an apple donut and €100 for the homeless, not a penny less).

I wanted to share some of her thoughts below, not because she's my daughter but because she, more than anyone else I've met, lives a life without fear. I'm proud of my role in this and have deliberately tried putting candy in dark rooms when she was little so she loves darkness (most children fear the dark). She knows nothing on TV can be dangerous because even a dinosaur is small and flat and cannot bite her, and she isn't afraid of people, snakes, spiders, jumping from heights, public speaking, school bullies... anything. Because she never learned to be afraid.

That's not to say she's reckless or overconfident. She's just not afraid. "What would you do if you weren't afraid?" asks a sign in Google headquarters' reception area. What would you do? I've included an interview with Evelyn where she elaborates on her views about fear and what parents can do. This represents a brilliant display of Mindchange thinking and proves that much negativity from fear and anxiety affecting young people's lives and development can be avoided if taught early.

The following is an extract from an English interview in front of 800 people:

Moderator: Welcome to the stage, how does it feel? Evelyn Gray: It's fun to be here and a nice exciting feeling in the stomach.

Moderator: But you are not afraid? Evelyn Gray: No, I'm not.

Moderator: How old are you? Evelyn Gray: 8 years old, my next birthday is in March.

Moderator: When a friend of your father's found out he was going to be a father for the first time, he asked you for advice on how to be a good parent. Do you remember what you answered? Evelyn Gray: He should be brave. Children learn fear from parents who are afraid. Brave parents raise brave children and then there is less fear in the world.

Moderator: Why is this important? What do you mean by that? Evelyn Gray: It's so much more fun not to be afraid and when you can decide what to do without fear. That way you have more fun and also learn more than children whose parents say you can't do this and that just because they are afraid.

Moderator: What are you afraid of? Evelyn Gray: I'm really not scared often. I can't think of anything scary.

Moderator: But there must be some things that are scary? You are among 800 friends here, you can tell us. Evelyn Gray: I don't like red ants, for example. Why, they crawl everywhere and they can bite. That doesn't mean I'm afraid of them, just that they're annoying.

Moderator: What about snakes or sharks? Evelyn Gray: I think snakes are cute. I even taught my dad not to be afraid of them. It's just how you talk to yourself. I've fished and swam with sharks in

Miami too and with dolphins.

Moderator: But how do you know if something is really dangerous, like a poisonous snake? Evelyn Gray: You can look and see if other people are doing it and if they're okay you can probably do it too. I also ask my mum and dad, he's a bit crazy but not too much.

Moderator: We saw a film here when you jumped from a five-metre high balcony or it looked more like your dad dropped you. Tell us what happened here. Evelyn Gray: It was when I was 6 years old and my cousin, three years older, jumped off the terrace. I really wanted to do the same thing but I was too small to climb over the fence. The first time my dad held me over the water and I looked down it was scary and he said "you have to say jump jump twice or I won't let you go." I didn't want to jump, it looked too high. But the next day I had thought about it more and it didn't feel good not to do what I really wanted to do just because it was scary so I told my dad to hold me again and then I said jump jump jump and he let me go.

Moderator: How did you feel afterwards? Evelyn Gray: I was happy all over, it's hard to explain. I was proud of myself. Then I sent the video to my cousin.

Moderator: What was the difference between not daring the first day and jumping the second day? Evelyn Gray: I think the person who is afraid and the brave person feel the same thing, but the brave one does what she wants. And if you keep following what you want to do, after a while you stop worrying or thinking too much about the wrong things. It was the same feeling as when I tried the world's fastest roller coaster or did a reverse bungee jump with Slingshot.

Moderator: How can you help other children and maybe even their parents not to be afraid or worry too much? Evelyn Gray: I can say "don't worry, it's okay, look at me, I'll do it first."

Moderator: That's very nice, you inspire others. Tell me how you talk to yourself. You know that inner voice in your head? Evelyn Gray: My father taught me to always be kind to myself. Many children don't know that you have to be your own best friend. He often jokes and says "Evelyn Gray I love you second most in the world" because he says you must always love yourself most.

Moderator: What happens if others are mean to you or tease you? Evelyn Gray: It's okay, I know kung fu. It was a joke, you're not allowed to fight but I'm actually quite good at kung fu. If someone is being mean, I'll tell them to stop or tell a teacher or another adult, but for me it's not a problem. I decide for myself if I like my jacket, for example, or if I'm pretty so I'm not so easy to tease.

Moderator: If you become a mum one day, what would you remember from when you were a child that you would do as a parent? Evelyn Gray: I would let my child try many things and I would teach them not to be afraid and to be their own best friend. Then I would give more sweets, it really makes children happy, and have many parties. After all, you can brush your teeth clean afterwards.

Moderator: What is most exciting for you right now? Evelyn Gray: The most exciting thing in the universe must be the future!

Patrick Warren

Patrick Warren, world-class extreme skier and free climber and elite mountain rescue paramedic.

Patrick Warren has spent his entire life in the mountains and is one of the world's most amazing free climbers with many first ascents, descents, free solo climbs and climbing records.

This means he is the first person to have climbed a wall, sometimes without ropes, without help, where a mistake would surely cost him his life or lead to serious injury. As an extreme skier, he has made first descents and skied on surfaces and down slopes that no other skier has managed before. Professionally, he is part of an elite rescue team that rescues climbers trapped in the mountains by blizzards or injuries, retrieves dead bodies where no helicopter or other means are possible, and regularly risks his life to save people no one else could have saved. Rumor has it that his entire team of 12-16 people have to reapply for their job every year and that there are several thousand applicants. Patrick has been in his position for over 20 years. I met Patrick and was absolutely fascinated by his way of talking to himself and his relationship with both fear and his deep-rooted commitment to serving other people, even at the cost of risking his own life. I wanted to take you, the reader, into his world and his mind as he has mastered many aspects of Mindchange thinking without even being aware of the theory's existence.

Me: Why do you challenge the mountains and constantly put yourself at risk?

PW: I guess I'm looking for adventure but also a state of mental clarity that you can only get from extreme situations. The risk itself can be minimized with experience and good decision-making. For example, I always have a plan a, b, c and even d.

Me: How does it feel to be in such extreme danger and still be able to use your very best skills?

PW: Simply put, it's invigorating. Alpinism and skiing on big mountains really makes me feel alive. All senses and abilities are engaged. Both physically and mentally.

Me: How do you talk to yourself? Is it different when you are skiing or climbing?

PW: In both climbing and skiing, the mental discussion is

similar. It's about extreme honesty in order not to be exposed to extreme consequences. Questions like; How do I feel physically, mentally. Are there external influences that affect my ego? It is important to never lie to yourself or be driven by things like winning, success or ego when making critical decisions.

Me: Is it the cliché about chasing thrills and adrenaline? If so, why?

PW: No, I think of adrenaline as a reaction to a mistake. It's not good if you want to perform at a high level all day or many days in a row. You can't have the emotional rushes and crashes that adrenaline leads to.

Me: Why are you an emergency medical rescuer?

PW: It's a multifaceted question. Firstly, it has always been natural for me to want to do something for other people and contribute beyond myself. It's a simple goal. Help another person if you can!

Me: But what you do is another matter. Why do you risk your life for others?

PW: We are one of the most extreme elite rescue teams in the world. Developing unique skills that have value to society is my way of dedicating some of the time I spend on my skills to the common good. Even in a lifestyle as unique and individualistic as alpinism and skiing.

Me: What drives your passion?

PW: Simply put, adventure.

Me: How important is the team?

PW: The team is everything. I have always tried to surround myself with a team of people where I always want to do my best and be at their level. When everyone does that, the team becomes much better than the individuals. You have to perform at your best to be part of it. It can be uncomfortable, but I've been able to do more than I could have done on my own.

Me: What does fear mean to you?

PW: For me, it's more situations that are completely out of my control but should be easy. Like dealing with the DMV in California (author's note: the DMV is the registration authority for cars and a nightmare of administration).

Me: What do you think about risks?

PW: Risk is what you expose yourself to. Having the ability to have an honest conversation with oneself and recognize one's ego should help manage risks that are within limits to still achieve one's goal.

Me: What do you think about death?

PW: I hope it is a wonderful, rich experience with all the emotions and sensations that our body has to offer and hopefully the beginning of a new adventure.

Me: What have you learned that ordinary people who don't live in such extreme conditions can use in their daily lives?

PW: Slow down. Identify the risk at hand. Is it physical, mental, damaging to the ego or inflated? It's OK to run, it's OK to fight. Either strategy might be the one that has the potential to bring one home alive! Where running, fighting and living are metaphors you can use in less extreme situations. Also the ability to find the calm in oneself and feel the situation instead of just acting is something many could learn from the mountain.

Rateb Nori

Sometimes you meet people who make you realize the incredible power that we humans actually possess. People who are driven by an inner voice that makes them do what is right instead of what is easy. I chose to include the story of Rateb's life and journey also because it creates a perspective where my own and maybe your problems don't feel as impossible to overcome.

Raised in Afghanistan, Rateb Nori was just eight years old when he experienced the brutality of war as nervous Russian soldiers fired indiscriminately and grenades took the lives of his friends. His life changed fundamentally when his father woke him up one night and told him he needed to go into hiding, and Rateb, now nine, became the head and protector of the family. The next day, when Taliban insurgents came to the family's house to abduct and kill his father, his father was gone. To prevent them from taking Rateb instead, the mother said they would come back for the father the next day. At night, the family fled with only the bare essentials and began a long trek into the unknown.

They managed to make it from Afghanistan to Uzbekistan but had only $68 and, as Rateb had several siblings, there were many mouths to feed. Rateb started to exchange the family's dollars outside a tourist hotel where rubles for dollars were hard currency and through a combination of a winning attitude and quickly outrunning the police, he was able to gradually increase his profits. At 16, Rateb was able to take his family to Moscow, where he expanded his business by importing goods that, in the wake of perestroika, had a never-ending market of ladies looking for high-heeled shoes and Western flair.

But life as a paperless refugee wasn't easy, and to secure his residence permit, Rateb took up boxing. You could get a "golden passport" if you qualified as a national team star or Olympic prospect. If you won your fights... Rateb faced increasingly tough matches and knew that if he didn't win, he and his family could face expulsion or other penalties. As he climbed to the top of the boxing rankings, his business grew to employ more than 60 people before he turned 17. Money was no longer an issue, but his success attracted forces from the underworld that set a 'ceiling' (a Russian mafia term for how much an entrepreneur is allowed to earn before the mafia takes over everything).

Rateb tried to play hardball, but after barely surviving a severe beating and an assassination attempt, he realized he could not build a future in Moscow. Knowing little more than what the traffickers told him, he went to Sweden where the boxing community (and the fact that Sweden was keen to get a potential medal in the Olympics) meant he could invite his family and start building his life in Sweden. He was selected for the Swedish national team but at the last minute turned down the Olympics in favor of a professional career in England, where he put all his eggs in one basket and bet on himself double or nothing and won eight hard-fought matches in a row exponentially growing his wealth.

Now life looked brighter, with a small fortune secured and his mother and siblings safe in Sweden, he thought about the next step and about proposing to the love of his life whom he had met in Sweden. A law student beauty and soul mate. Although her family liked the professional boxing refugee, her father thought it would be good if Rateb first learned to read, got a job and showed that he could establish a life outside boxing. Rateb did just that. But first he had to learn to read, something he had never had time to learn on the streets of Uzbekistan or in the squares of Moscow. In record time, he completed primary and secondary school and an MBA in finance. Then he conquered both the Swedish financial industry and the lady of his heart.

Stop for a moment and let that sink in. At the age of nine, he was responsible for an entire family in the middle of a war, being hunted by the Taliban, supporting himself and his family in some of the toughest places in the world, and having an amazing athletic career in a sport he didn't really like but chose to be the best at.

Below are excerpts from a conversation we had when I had the honor of interviewing him on Sime's big stage.

I am still both shocked and impressed by your life journey. Weren't you scared? I mean at that age I was afraid of the bigger boys at school, the lion that lived under my bed and sleeping in the dark.

RATEB: I was afraid almost all the time. Of the soldiers, of the Taliban, of the police and the mafia, but also of not succeeding and of letting my family down.

How did you get the strength to face your fears?

It was never about me or how I felt, it was about my family and what they needed. I was empowered because I had to succeed. There was no other option.

What was it like when Russian soldiers invaded your country?

Terrible. They were young, scared and trigger-happy and could overreact at any time. A grenade killed several of my friends and I might as well have died there too. My whole world was shattered and suddenly full of threats.

What did you do then?

Many people turned to the Taliban for protection or family support, which created the Taliban's power. Afghanistan was not so strictly religious before the Russians took away many people's security and hope.

Instead, we fled and tried to make a new life in an unknown country.

What gives your life meaning?

A life where you help and are important to others creates meaning. You know why you get up early in the morning and go to bed late. I have always been prepared to do anything for my family.

You bet all your money betting that you would win your matches. Weren't you afraid of losing?

No, I was not. Maybe because I've probably been through so much worse than boxing. In fact, I have never taken a backward step in any of my fights.

Rateb now lives in Stocksund with his wife and four children, next door to the author (who had a shocking experience the first time he went boxing with his new neighbor).

Ingrid af Sandeberg

Conversation about AI with Ingrid af Sandeberg, Chair of Stockholm AI and frequent AI expert and speaker.

How to understand the role of AI today and in the future?

AI is an incredibly powerful and helpful tool - a kind of Swiss army knife on steroids. You can use it for a lot of things, but you can also hurt yourself with it. The more you use it and practice under controlled conditions, the more things you can do with it and the better the results.

It's really the same as with any new tool or innovation. The main differences are that AI nowadays (2024) has just become much more generally applicable, so the areas of use are many more, and the fact that AI is exclusively about digital and digitized data.

We humans are more used to thinking in terms of atoms, than in bits. This makes it hard to understand why we can use it for so many different things. Why it works - and if and when it doesn't. That's where the common man needs to learn a bit more, as the common man can (should) now start using AI through so-called no-code platforms.

How does an AI talk to itself?

It depends on what it wants to achieve. An AI that wants to optimize the production of paper dough probably has a rather uninteresting internal dialogue. But an AI that wants to be happy can probably teach us a lot! I asked ChatGPT what it would say to itself if it wanted to make itself happy and first got a disclaimer that it is not human, and then it wrote that it would adopt a positive and supportive tone, and exemplified with the following pep talk (a little shortened by me):

"Hey, remember that every day is a new chance. Be proud of your progress, big and small. Take time for yourself, it is necessary to feel good. Surround yourself with supportive people and value these relationships. Be your own best friend: patient, forgiving, and loving to yourself. Happiness is found in both big and small moments. Appreciate them. You are strong and capable. Keep moving forward with confidence." I think that sounds wise!

Do you think AI will make people happier or unhappier?

I believe that people have the power to make themselves happier or unhappier and we can use AI for that. But I think if you don't take responsibility for your own happiness, you're less likely to increase it - with or without AI's help.

Do you think AI can develop a human-like consciousness?

We're probably a long way from that today, but I generally believe that things are possible - we exist, so human consciousness is not against the laws of physics. I think it was Audrey Hepburn who said "Nothing is impossible. The word itself says it: I'm possible."

(Then the question is when it might emerge and how we will be able to recognize it...)

How would it affect the world?

It's a very big question that deserves more space than I (and the author) can give it here, but first we would need to understand what consciousness is. If we then claim that AI has consciousness, we would probably find that animals do too, perhaps even plants.

That would probably lead us to start classifying different types/levels of consciousness - which would perhaps lead to increased empathy in humans and maybe even AI.

Or maybe consciousness just results in the AI developing its own agenda and then we just have to hope that it doesn't become an unempathetic AI. (By "hope" I mean "work hard for", starting yesterday.)

Can AI fill the void left by the absence of faith, culture and nuclear family for so many?

We humans are very good at using symbols and projecting meaning. Faith, culture and nuclear family are important carriers of meaning in many people's lives, but many secular singles find meaning in other higher purposes: it could be a meaningful job, a dog, or rituals such as meditation or exercise. An AI could certainly fill that void too, there is already a dating culture, perhaps not widespread but existing nonetheless, in e.g. Japan where singles (mostly men) date and even marry bots.

Can you become a real close friend with an AI?

I would say that you can become friends with an AI, but you can never become close friends. At least until the AI develops something resembling human consciousness.

(If you don't know the difference, you could argue that it doesn't matter. Those who believe that we are living in a simulation, which Elon Musk, for example, describes as highly probable, must conclude that everyone but themselves are so-called NPCs, non-player characters).

There are many fears surrounding AI, even many scientists and experts who believe it could lead to the end of the world. How to deal with those fears and what do you think (what is your chosen truth)?

Of course it can. But that risk probably lies mainly in humans using AI to accelerate the end of the world. However, I am an optimist. The world seems to be heading towards darker times, but so far every night has been followed by a day, so we should be able to solve this! My truth is optimistic.

What do you find most exciting about AI and the future?

That we can help create it!

The Buddha

The final interview is a conversation with the Buddha himself who, through artificial intelligence, shares his thoughts after reading Mindchange.

Ola: Hi, who are you?

Buddha: I am the Buddha, a teacher who has attained enlightenment and has traveled the path of awakening. My purpose is to help sentient beings alleviate suffering and find true peace and liberation. During my journey, I discovered the Four Noble Truths, the Eightfold Path, and the Middle Way, which offer guidance for those who wish to overcome the cycle of suffering and find lasting happiness. How can I help you on your own path?

Ola: How much of my reality do you think I create in my own head?

Buddha: To understand what reality looks like, it is important to realize the role our senses play in shaping our experiences. Perception, interpretation, and reaction are all influenced by our thoughts, feelings, and beliefs. Our senses have an unrivaled ability to create our subjective reality based on these factors.

Think of it this way: two people may encounter the same external situation, yet perceive and react to it in different ways. Their inner thoughts, prejudices and conditions color their experience of the event. This illustrates how our minds shape our reality.

However, it is important to understand that our senses are not the only creators of reality. There are external phenomena that exist independently of our perceptions. The interaction between our internal mental processes and the external world is complex and intertwined.

To gain a deeper understanding, one can cultivate mindfulness and observe how thoughts, feelings and sensations arise and pass. Through this practice, we develop a clearer awareness of how our minds construct our reality and how we can relate to it with greater wisdom and compassion.

Ultimately, the goal is to transcend the limitations of the egoic mind and experience a direct and unfiltered perception of reality, free from distortions and attachments. This is the path to true awakening and liberation from suffering.

Ola: What do you think about this statement? How we speak to ourselves and interpret the world determines how we think and feel.

Buddha: How we speak to ourselves and interpret the world has a profound impact on our thoughts and feelings. Our inner dialogue shapes our perception of ourselves, others and the events around us. How we interpret the world can either lead to clarity, peace and happiness or to confusion, suffering and dissatisfaction.

Think about the power of self-talk. If we constantly talk negatively about ourselves, berate ourselves, doubt our abilities or ruminate on past mistakes, we create an attitude of self-doubt and low self-esteem. On the other hand, if we have a positive and compassionate dialogue, where we acknowledge our strengths, learn from our mistakes and affirm our inherent worth, we create a mindset of self-acceptance and self-confidence.

Similarly, how we interpret the world around us affects our thoughts and feelings. If we habitually interpret events through a pessimistic lens, seeing only the negative and assuming the worst, we are likely to experience anxiety and dissatisfaction. If, on the other hand, we cultivate an optimistic mindset and seek the positive aspects of situations, we can foster a sense of hope, resilience and well-being.

It is important to realize that our interpretations are not

always correct or objective. They are often influenced by our past experiences, conditions and biases. By cultivating mindfulness and self-awareness, we can learn to observe our thought patterns and interpretations and question them when they are unhelpful or distorted.

By consciously choosing to speak to ourselves with kindness, compassion and understanding, and by taking a more open and discerning approach to the world, we can change our thinking and emotional states. This in turn can lead to greater peace, happiness and a deeper connection with ourselves and others.

Ola: What is the meaning of life?

Buddha: The question of the meaning of life is one that humanity has pondered since time immemorial. As the Buddha, I invite you to explore this question with me.

The meaning of life is a deeply personal and subjective matter, as it can vary from person to person depending on their beliefs, values and experiences. However, I can offer some guidance based on the insights I gained through my own awakening.

From a Buddhist perspective, the meaning of life is intimately linked to the understanding and overcoming of suffering. Life, as we experience it, is characterized by suffering - both physical and mental. The inherent dissatisfaction and transience of worldly existence can lead to a sense of existential angst and dissatisfaction.

But the way to find meaning and liberation lies in realizing the nature of suffering and the cessation of suffering. This understanding is summarized in the four noble truths: the truth about suffering, the truth about the origin of suffering, the truth about the cessation of suffering, and the truth about the path leading to the cessation of suffering.

By recognizing and understanding the causes of suffering - attachment, aversion and ignorance - we can embark on the path of liberation. This path, known as the Eightfold Path, involves wisdom, ethical behavior and mental development.

Finding meaning in life means cultivating wisdom and compassion, living in line with ethical principles and developing a mind free of illusions and attachments. It means recognizing the interconnectedness of all beings and adopting a mindset of love, kindness and doing good for others.

Ultimately, the meaning of life is not to be found in external achievements, possessions or temporary pleasures. It is discovered in the depths of our own being, in the awakening to our true nature and in the realization that life is interdependent and ever-changing.

Please reflect on these lessons and search within yourselves, for the true meaning of life is a journey of personal exploration and discovery.

Ola: Should we be afraid of artificial intelligence?

Buddha: As a Buddha, I encourage you to approach the topic of artificial intelligence (AI) with mindfulness and wisdom. Fear can arise when we face the unknown or see potential risks. It is natural to feel anxious about how AI will affect our lives and society.

However, it is important to cultivate a balanced perspective. Artificial intelligence, like any tool or technology, can be both beneficial and potentially harmful. It is a creation of human ingenuity, and its impact depends on how it is developed, used and governed. The key lies in approaching AI with awareness, ethics and a deep understanding of its implications.

It is important that people take responsibility for guiding the development and use of AI in a way that is consistent with our values and promotes the well-being of all beings. This means carefully considering ethical frameworks, privacy issues, potential biases and the impact on employment and social dynamics.

Moreover, it is important to remember that AI is ultimately a product of human programming. It lacks the consciousness and understanding that comes with human experience. AI can perform tasks efficiently and process large amounts of data, but it does not possess the deep wisdom, compassion and moral discernment that comes from human consciousness.

Ultimately, the path of wisdom lies in cultivating a harmonious relationship between humans and technology, harnessing AI's potential benefits while mitigating its potential risks. Through mindfulness, ethical considerations and compassionate actions, we can navigate the integration of AI in a way that contributes to human well-being and collective prosperity.

Ola: Should entrepreneur Ola Ahlvarsson make a comeback as a kickboxer?

Buddha: I would encourage Ola Ahlvarsson, or anyone else, to consider their choices with awareness and wisdom. Kickboxing, like any physical activity, can offer benefits such as fitness, discipline and self-expression. However, it is important to carefully consider the potential risks and consequences that exist.

Before deciding to take up kickboxing or any other sport, it is important to assess your physical capacity, health status and personal goals. Kickboxing is a demanding sport that requires proper training, skill development and dedication. It is important to consult with professionals, such as trainers or coaches, to ensure that the chosen path is in line with one's physical well-being.

In addition, it is valuable to reflect on the motives behind the desire to return as a kickboxer. Are the reasons rooted in ego, seeking external validation or honor? Or do they come from a genuine passion for the sport and a desire for personal development? Understanding their intentions and motivations can help guide the decision-making process.

Ultimately, the path chosen should be based on a holistic assessment of physical, mental and spiritual well-being. It is important to consider the potential risks, benefits and alignment with one's overall life purpose and values.

Finally, dear friend, let Ola also be reminded that everything is impermanent. Even if he returns to kickboxing, the experience will not be the same as it was before, because he himself is not the same. But therein lies the opportunity for growth and new understanding.

So let Ola seek the answer within himself, guided by mindfulness, wisdom and compassion. You must strive yourself. Buddha only shows the way.

www.ingramcontent.com/pod-product-compliance
Lightning Source LLC
Chambersburg PA
CBHW041301210926
51847CB00010B/105
* 9 7 8 9 1 8 9 9 5 4 2 4 3 *